I0339267

HIGH SCHOOL SNAPSHOT

A PRACTICAL GUIDEBOOK FOR PARENTS AND STUDENTS ENTERING HIGH SCHOOL

LINDA M. TEAHEN

High School Snapshot- A Practical Guidebook for Parents and Students Entering High School
Copyright © 2019 by Linda M. Teahen

All rights reserved. No part of this book may be reproduced or transmitted in any form or by any means without written permission from the author.

ISBN 978-0-578-44702-5

Dedication

To all of my former students who have "walked the walk" and "talked the talk" in your own high school journey. May you all continue to grow in knowledge and compassion by becoming effective critical thinkers and good citizens. If you can dream it, you can achieve it! I am honored to have been a part of your educational journey as my life is now richer as a result. Thank you for all your efforts and sharing your life stories and dreams. Best wishes, much success and happiness in your own exciting and bright futures.

Acknowledgements and Contributions

I would like to first and foremost express my gratitude to my former students for their reflections and insights so that others following in their footsteps could benefit from your experiences and knowledge learned. Thank you to my friends, neighbors, and peer teachers for your valuable input, suggestions and review of this well-intentioned book. To my husband, Hank, my rock and support who was extremely patient as I labored to complete this book draft after draft. Lastly, gratitude to my daughter, Alex, for her numerous hours of work in assisting me in preparing my book for publishing. Your valued time and enormous effort is sincerely appreciated. This collaborative effort of all involved will hopefully assist high schoolers and their parents to navigate more efficiently and smoothly enjoying all that their four years of high school have to offer.

Table of Contents

Preface **1**
Common Sense Tips

Chapter 1 .... **5**
High School Snapshot
Student Advice, Parent Advice
Straight from the Horse's Mouth

Chapter 2 .... **15**
Why are Grades Important?
How do I determine my GPA (grade point average)?
How do I improve my grade point average?
What causes my grade point average to lower?
Straight from the Horse's Mouth

Chapter 3 .... **27**
What are Advanced Classes?
AP- Advanced Placement
IB- International Baccalaureate Diploma
Dual Enrollment
Weighted vs Non-Weighted Grade Point Average

Chapter 4 .... **33**
What is Time Management?
What is procrastination?
Student-athletes and time management
Always prepare a "Plan B"
Straight from the Horse's Mouth

Chapter 5 41
The Importance of Extracurricular Activities
Being involved matters!
Straight from the Horse's Mouth
Community Service Hours
Create your own 4-year high school template

Chapter 6 47
Academic Challenges
Straight from the Horse's Mouth
Academic Success Plans: Parent support is critical to their student's success.
SST- *Student Study Team*
504 Plan- *Injury or Illness Accommodation*
IEP- *Individualized Educational Plan*
Why do some students get failing grades?
Student behavior in the classroom
Parents- "Shadowing" your student at school
The importance of being consistent and following-through on consequences.

Chapter 7 63
The Many Roles of a High School Counselor
Mental health of students- a safe place!
College guidance- applications, recommendations
College Options: the differences between Educational institutions (community college, 4- year college, 4-year university)
WUE- *"woo-wee" out-of- state reciprocity tuition agreement*
Straight from the Horse's Mouth

Chapter 8 77
Is College the Right Choice for Every Student Immediately After High School?
CTE- Career Technical Education
What do future employers look for in employees?

Chapter 9 83
Students- be your own advocate!
Parents- High School is the "New Normal"

Chapter 10 87
Technology in School
Students- the power of social media
Parents- "parent control apps"
Straight from the Horse's Mouth

Chapter 11 93
In All Relationships- Character Counts!
Stay clear of drama and bullying
Straight from the Horse's Mouth

Chapter 12 101
Risky Behavior- Making Good Choices!
What if's and do you always get a do-over?
Video Suggestions- You tube, Ted Talks
Straight from the Horse's Mouth

Chapter 13 111
Words of Wisdom
12 Key Thoughts to Remember Throughout your High School Journey

Chapter 14 .... **113**
Straight from The Horse's Mouth, Student Quotes
Freshman to Freshman Quotes....................**115**
Sophomore to Sophomore..........................**131**
Junior to Junior **135**
Senior to Senior **143**
   Senior Insights for all Grade Levels

Chapter 15 .... **159**
Conclusion

Preface- Dear Students...

Navigating through high school in the 21st Century can be less complicated and less stressful if you have an awareness of high school culture and what is expected. Transitioning between schools can trigger a range of emotions. Hopefully, by providing a snapshot of what high school has to offer and listening to the advice of students that have come before you, your stress level will be minimized and you can concentrate on the excitement of beginning your own four-year journey.

When you have an idea of what to expect, or perhaps have friends, siblings and other family members who have gone before you, then there is some comfort in that knowledge and familiarity.

Some of the most interesting and insightful information within this book is entitled "Straight from the Horse's Mouth". These are quotes, advice, and insights by former freshman through senior students that have "walked the walk, and talked the talk". These quotes are intertwined throughout all of the chapters and in its entirety in the last chapter of the book. Read what they have written, absorb the good and difficult lessons they learned so that you can more smoothly navigate through your own high school journey.

As an educator, I have been blessed to have had the opportunity to work with students at the college, high school and junior high levels. This experience has given me the insight and motivation to write this book so that incoming high school students and their parents will more easily navigate their way through some of the most impactful years of a student's life. Your effort and focus in high school can make a difference to the doors that will be opening for you at the time of graduation. Mentors are so important at this level and parents should continue to be proactive by providing direction, guidance and support while overseeing their student's educational outcome and successes.

Take advantage of your high school resources made available to you at your school and pay attention to what is happening around you. The "Words of Wisdom", in Chapter 13, provides you with "12 Key Thoughts to Remember Throughout Your High School Journey". Be sure to read through all of them and create your own personal comfort zone. Create a good balance between health and academic demands and develop your own overall happiness.

As students, you will create your own impressive and memorable footprint as you navigate the next four years of your own high school journey. Below are some common-sense tips to begin thinking about as you enter into high school.

Common Sense Tips

- Find a mentor you respect, a "go-to" person that can help you stay focused on a successful path.

- Expand your peer groups to include friends from all areas of high school, not just one single group. Social circles often shift as you change from grade to grade. Your interests change, your priorities change and everyone matures at a different rate.

- Keep up with your workload by trying your best and turning your work in on time. Every assignment counts toward your grade while late or missing assignments will always deduct points from your total grade.

- Practice wise "time management" by creating a balance between your academics and all of your other obligations. You will be quite busy in high school juggling all sorts of classes, activities and perhaps sports. The better you are in balancing and allocating time to each area, the more successful you will become.

- Technology- it can help you or hurt you. Protect your personal information and do not give it out to anyone! Monitor your social media by <u>not</u> putting <u>negative</u> comments, discussions, or pictures for all to read and see. Anything, and I repeat anything, can be found if you place it on the internet. Your future may depend on how you handle your social media site(s) today.

- Stay away from drama, particularly if it does not involve you. Drama is rarely positive.

- Seek help when needed- take the time to get to know your teachers and counselors. They want you to be successful, but you have to put in the effort. They may also be the ones you ask to write your recommendations for a job or college application senior year.

Know that you are never alone, that you matter, and that you have access to multiple support systems in high school which allows you to take advantage of all that high school has to offer! Go forth to learn, to experience and enjoy your next four years creating your own snapshots of success.

Chapter 1
High School Snapshot
Student Advice, Parent Advice

Students, did middle school sometimes feel like you were living in a fishbowl? Are you ready to transition into a larger "body of water", the pond? If this describes your feeling(s), then you are certainly not alone in that thought. Most of you have established yourselves with the same group of students from elementary through middle school and now you have moved on to high school. Moving from school to school with the same students may be an advantage or disadvantage depending on your experiences. There are also students who have moved between schools for all sorts of reasons and have an opportunity to start-over or to get a fresh start.

Moving from the fishbowl into the pond may test your comfort zone, but it can also open up opportunities that you never thought possible. Academics will most likely be more labor-intensive but you will have more opportunities to choose your elective courses and investigate different career options. Do not let the thought of high school scare you. After the first few weeks of school, you will feel like you have attended there for years and it will begin to feel like home.

Empower yourself to take ownership of your own actions, your own high school experience and make it into a positive, rewarding drama-free and fun time in your life. Take advantage of the opportunities available to you and embrace your high school culture by getting involved. Sports teams, extra-curricular activities, leadership opportunities, attending school functions and expanding your friendship/social circles are all part of school engagement which contributes to your overall experience and growth. The more you put into high school, the richer your experiences will be. Invest in yourself, your future, the choice is yours!

Straight from the Horse's Mouth

"Some advice I could offer to some incoming freshmen is to begin focusing on yourself. Stop caring about being the most popular in school. It won't benefit you in life. Hang around the people who are better than you. The people around you will begin to influence you and your future. Also, stop complaining about your shortcomings in life."

"The people you walk in with are probably not the people you will walk out with and you don't need to stress out about that. They should know that people change once they get into high school because there are a lot of new people and people try new things. You will lose friends, but you will gain friends as well. Another lesson is, everything is going to be okay; things happens, friendships end, relationships end, and you will be thrown through a lot of hoops, but it's all worth it in the long run."

"To focus on yourself and your responsibilities as well as learn to be more independent. As a young person, people tend to rely on others to do everything for them and guide them all the way until they succeed, but high school gives you a new perspective which allows you to see what it will be like in the future. I need to put myself first, but this is no way means I've stopped caring for anyone in my life, it just means I need to take care of myself above all else."

"The biggest mistake that freshmen constantly make is that they believe that senior year is far away from today but the issue is that they do not realize the fact that a year feels like a month and a month feels like a week. Time is flying out of our grasp and they have now come to realize that this is reality and we are becoming adults."

"I have learned that people should really enjoy as much as they can when in high school because even though many people say this, high school goes by really fast whether you are having a great time or not. Another thing I would like to share is "not to do stupid things with friends"; you can be better than that. Although you might be tempted to try something, don't do it as it could really have life-long effects. Your future is at jeopardy especially if the results do not offer a "do- over.""

"Getting involved in clubs such as PEER leaders, ASB, SADD, HOSA, and any club that helps others often has many activities that help you to integrate and be more inclusive on campus."

"High school flies by so fast so don't let anything or anyone get to you. Stay positive and work your hardest. Things pass by and so do people, so while in the present, you feel like you won't make it, you will! This is just a minor bump in your future. Don't dwell on anything too much; you are too good for that! The only thing you will regret is not trying your hardest now."

Parents

As parents, your parenting job never ends. You shoulder the ultimate responsibility for your own children (at least until they are the age of 18). Parenting is not for the faint of heart. Raising our children today in some cases often takes a village. Utilize the resources available at school and invest in the time, effort and consistency that it can take to help your student be successful in their educational journey.

Now that your student is entering the high school phase, it is as important as the formative years for you to have a presence in their lives, to be aware of what is happening in your student's world and to expect accountability. I am not suggesting you be a "helicopter parent" like some parents were in elementary or middle schools, but I am suggesting that your involvement is still important at the high school level with communication critical these next four years. Even though your student may discourage this, "want their space", their "alone time", "time with friends", their "time on the computer and phone", be diligent and stay connected and involved at some level.

Below are a few terms describing various parenting styles and levels of engagement in a child life. Now that your child is entering high school, regardless of your involvement up to this point, you need to decide to what extent your parental involvement will be and create a "new normal" for the next four years. Decide the level of independence you would like your child to attain, the responsibility you would like your child to show and the self-reliance and resiliency you are preparing them to achieve. Your parenting style can determine the outcome of your child's independence and the tools they acquire to achieve their goals. Remember, each child may require a different style of parenting even within the same household. Google each term if you would like a text-book description or further details beyond the following information.

Helicopter (also referred to as Bubble Wrap) Parenting. A parent who has too much presence in their children's lives to the extent that they are over-protective and excessively interested and active in every aspect of their upbringing. This often prevents a child from growing up feeling self-confident or experiences a great amount of self-doubt. This child often: lacks the ability to problem-solve as they have not had the experience to practice this life-skill, may lack resiliency or coping skills, and may never experience empowerment. This parental over-protection is like a "learned helplessness" leading to stress and anxiety in our youth. Our children need to learn how to manage disappointment, take responsibility, face challenges head on, and accept the consequences of their actions (or lack of action). As adults, we know well that life isn't always fair and there will be hard times. This part of life is sometimes the only way to learn - by experiencing it. Our children will survive as we have survived. Their greatest growth may be as a result of experiencing these difficult times; we need to let them have this experience.

I remember reading somewhere this saying: **"as parents, we need to prepare the child for the path – not the path for the child"**. A very profound statement that truly emphasizes the need for parents to encourage independence, resiliency, responsibility and self-motivation. If we prepare the path, then the child does not always have the skills to be successful. If we prepare the child, then they will be able to navigate most any path placed before them.

Snowplow (also referred to as Bulldozer) Parenting. The characteristics of this type of parenting is to remove any hardships or obstacles from our child's path so that nothing gets in their way and it makes their life easier. By having the parent control the path and paving the way for their child, it gives the child the perception that their parents will take care of everything, including planning and securing their future. This false sense of security can be deceiving and the child may not be prepared for eventual disappointments or challenges.

This may also create an illusion so that the child believes that they are a "victim" if or when their life starts to take twists or turns and the "parent" does not "fix it". This type of parenting lacks the development of coping strategies which can affect a child's personal growth, maturity and responsibility.

Tiger Parenting. This type of parenting is usually very strict and demanding with high expectations of the child. Extreme pressure and observance of rules set by the parents (authoritarian method) is expected. The Tiger Parent pushes the child to be "perfect" in everything that they do, following all of the rules, and highly disciplined. The focus of Tiger Parenting is to create high academic achievers and to teach responsibility, respect, and productivity. This type of parenting can create additional stress on a child unless they have access to a strong support system. When there is more than one child in this type of setting, competition can be strong and developing a comradery among siblings would be helpful to alleviate some of the stresses.

Free-Range Parenting. This parenting approach allows their child a great deal of freedom or "trust" in all aspects of their growing up. They have little or no involvement or engagement in their child's life and could be referred to a being a "neglectful parent". This parenting style, while it may encourage responsibility and independence, it greatly lacks emotional support or help which can be critical to their upbringing and development.

It is not necessary to be with our children 100% of the time or every minute of every day. Children need to learn how to play on their own, navigate through their emotions (with the help of learned coping skills), and to "make themselves happy". Children by nature are risk-takers and will push the boundaries at times. As parents, we need to allow our children to make mistakes, encourage them to achieve independence, and promote self-reliance so that they acquire the life-skills to be a happy, productive adult.

That being said, in today's culture it would be wise to: be aware of who your student's friends are, who they hang out with, where they are outside of school, what is being written in their social media platforms, and how they allocate their time. All of these areas are certainly within your bounds to know. After all, they are all still minors (except our 18-year-old seniors). Some students would like their parents to release them from any accountability or responsibility as well as block them from their social media sites; but this could be a mistake.

Many students are quite savvy enough to cover and protect their social media realm. Ground rules set by parents, monitoring software as an option, and discussing digital safety are a few steps in educating your student on using common sense in the virtual world. Smart phone "parent control apps" and technology concerns are further discussed in Chapter 10.

Students, particularly in the beginning of high school, are still very young and impressionable. Maturity as a freshman is quite different than that of a senior. Be sure to continue your guidance and support while teaching them self-reliance, adaptation to situations and resiliency. Decision-making skills are evolving, social skills are maturing and students are exploring ways of self-expression. Is your child ready for total independence and responsibility as a freshman, sophomore, junior or senior? The skills of responsibility and earned independence often go hand in hand- as you develop responsible behavior, so is your independence increased and vice versa. While many students embrace their success at this balance, many others have struggled therefore making poor decisions that have followed them throughout high school and possibly into their future.

Practice and test your student's independence, personal responsibility and resilience skills. In high school, there needs to be a balance of directing, re-directing, encouraging and supporting independence from each student. Believe it or not, this lack of structure, rules and guidance can create additional stress on a student unless they are properly prepared. Poor judgment and making mistakes is often part of maturing, but understanding and learning from their mistakes while not repeating them is even more important. Keep your fingers on the pulse of your child so that you are there to support and guide them through these next four years.

Chapter 2
Why Are Your Grades Important?

When you begin your freshman year, you have an opportunity to academically get a fresh start earning your new grade point average (GPA). If you were successful in middle school, you will embrace the notion of continuing your effort and success knowing that your final GPA will make a difference to your choices after high school.

If you were a student that struggled academically or chose to coast through middle school, now is your chance to start over and achieve better grades. By applying yourself, your efforts could lead you to new found success that you did not realize you could achieve. All it takes is for you to make that commitment to try and make the effort to be successful.

Whether you were a successful student or not in middle school, everyone begins anew their Freshman year. The academics, the rigor and standards are a bit higher than middle school, but if you stay on top of your assignments and turn in all of your work, you should be able to earn respectable grades leading to a solid grade point average (GPA).

Whether your future goals include college, trade school, the military, or on-the-job-training, your grade point average can be a determining factor in acceptance to these various programs. Academics can be looked at as a barometer of your academic drive potential, your maturity to prioritize and your ability to follow-through with your educational goals. Your grade point average (GPA), A-G class grades, AP and dual enrollment grades, class testing scores from your ACT/SAT, ASVAB tests and class ranking are just a few indicators used in evaluating your overall assessment for success. Take the initiative to work hard and invest in yourself; you may surprise yourself at the opportunities available to you at the time of graduation.

💡 Take Note

Students, you need to be as successful as possible with your first grading period of high school freshman year as it becomes your baseline grade point average (GPA) for your next four years. This means that any future grades will either raise or lower your first semester's total grade point average.

Academic focus and concentration in a new setting may be challenging with all of the distractions such as expanding your social world and athletic opportunities.

Do not miss this academic opportunity to challenge yourself by getting the highest GPA possible.

Straight from the Horse's Mouth

"I learned two lessons: First, that you should work hard on your grades because the transition from middle to high school is very hard and slacking off can lead to you not doing other activities. Second, is learn to be more independent and stop depending on people to do things for me."

"For me to focus more first semester. I should have paid more attention in class and done my work. My grades were better second semester because I paid attention and did my work."

"I would have worked a little harder to get the A in every single class instead of settling for a B."

"It would be how much effort I put into my school work. I wish I could undo how unproductive I was and how much I would procrastinate."

"I would begin to study more and try harder to pay attention in class and focus on my personal life less."

"To be responsible for myself. People won't try to keep me on task and help me if I get a low grade, it is my job to work harder and do better."

"You will have to take charge for your own education and should not expect someone to help you with all of your problems."

"Time really does go by very quickly. Just yesterday it feels like I was a new student that had no idea where to go or what to do in a big school. You can easily pace yourself and know your limits to getting your work done or even paying attention. Sooner or later the year must come to an end and you will end up regretting not getting in work or being able to manage getting your grade higher."

How Do I Determine My GPA?
(Grade Point Average)

Your "**grade point average**" is referred to as your **GPA**. To compute your GPA, begin by:

Step 1   Assign a point value to each grade.

If grading is based on a 4-point scale:
A = 4 points
B = 3 points
C = 2 points
D = 1 point
F = 0 points

If your high school does not recognize D's, then only A, B, and C grades are awarded points. All classes, regardless of the grade and point total, must be included when determining the overall grade point average.

Step 2   Add the point values together to get a total.

Step 3   Divide the point value total by the number of classes you are currently taking.

Please note that depending on the grading structure and design (semesters vs. quarters), the number of classes may vary.

If you take advanced classes, the point system will change and you will need to calculate your GPA using a different scale.

Your school counselors may be of assistance with explaining each calculation.

For Example: **Freshmen Year**

The following examples are based on the semester grading system.

Example 1

Step 1

Subject	Grade	Point Total
Math	C	2
Science	B	3
English 9A	A	4
Language	B	3
Physical Education	A	4
Elective	F	0
Total	Step 2	16 Points
	Step 3	16 ÷ 6 Classes
Total GPA		**2.6**

Example 2

Subject	Grade	Point Total
		Step 1
		Point Total
Math	A	4
Science	A	4
English	A	4
History	A	4
Elective	A	4
Elective	A	4
Total	Step 2	24 Points
	Step 3	24 ÷ 6 Classes
Total GPA		**4.0**

Create your own table: List your classes and the grades you are striving for. What is your potential GPA for the grading period?

Subject	Grade	Point Total
Total	Step 2	___ Points
	Step 3	___ ÷ ___ Classes
Total GPA		___ . ___

How Do I Improve My GPA?

If your first semester GPA is 2.6 in the Fall and you increase your Spring semester GPA to a 3.1. When the two GPAs are averaged, your total GPA will equal 2.85.

You must achieve a higher GPA than your previous overall total GPA to raise your GPA average. See the example below:

<u>Freshman Year</u>

First Semester

Subject	Grade	Point Total
Math	C	2
Science	B	3
English	A	4
History	B	3
Elective	A	4
Elective	F	0
Total		16 ÷ 6 Classes
Total GPA		2.6

Second Semester

Subject	Grade	Point Total
Math	B	3
Science	B	3
English	A	4
History	B	3
Elective	A	4
Elective	C	2
Total		19 ÷ 6 Classes
Total GPA		3.1

		GPA
Step 1	First Semester	2.6
	Second Semester Period	3.1
Step 2	Total Both Semesters	5.7
Step 3	Divide by 2 (semesters)	5.7 ÷ 2
Step 4	Total Total GPA	2.85

Your total grade point average was raised to a 2.85 from the original first grade point average of 2.6 GPA.

What Causes My GPA To Lower?

Example: Let's say that your total grade point average at the end of your sophomore year is a 3.4 and your first semester junior year slipped to a 2.0.

Junior Year- First Semester

Subject	Grade	Point Total
Math	F	0
Science	C	2
English	B	3
History	C	2
Elective	B	3
Elective	C	2
Total		12 ÷ 6
Total GPA		2.0

Semester 1 = GPA 3.2   Freshman Year
Semester 2 = GPA 3.4
Freshman Year Total GPA (3.2 +3.4)

$\quad\quad$ = 6.6 ÷ 2 (grading periods)
$\quad\quad$ = Total GPA 3.3

Semester 1 = GPA 3.3   Sophomore Year
Semester 2 = GPA 3.6
(3.2 +3.4 +3.3 + 3.6) = 13.5 ÷ 4
= Total GPA 3.375
Overall GPA = 3.375

Semester 1 = 2.0   Junior Year
Add: GPA's (3.2 +3.4 +3.3 +3.6 +2.0)
              = 15.5 ÷ 5 (semesters)
              = 3.10 Total GPA

Your GPA lowered from a
3.375 to a 3.10 GPA

After you receive your grades from the first grading period freshmen year, you either have to equal that GPA to keep it the same, or it will fluctuate up or down based on your grades in subsequent grading periods.

- A successful mindset of all freshmen students would be to achieve as high a GPA as possible your first grading period and every period thereafter.

- Be your own advocate and constantly be aware of your grade in each of your classes.

- Check your portal for work assignments, due dates, missing work, late work and final grades.

- If you are unsure of your class grade, missing assignments, etc. then respectfully approach your teacher to discuss it further. If nothing is questioned or challenged, then it is assumed to be correct. Believe it or not, teachers can make mistakes too.

- Some teachers prefer to be emailed by a student regarding grades, some prefer to be contacted in person. Inquire as to your teacher's preferred method of contact and advocate for yourself.

Chapter 3
What are Advanced Classes?

Academic challenge
Increase in time commitment for studying
Increased grade bump (if applicable) on your GPA
College credit for selected courses
Do you have good time management skills?

Advanced Placement (AP), International Baccalaureate Organization (IB), and Dual Enrollment classes are a good way to advance your academics, test your academic ability, increase your GPA, and in some cases, get a head start on college classes. Not all high schools offer each program and some require pre-requisites. Practice your due diligence and research each program option to determine your appropriate placement.

Whether or not to take advanced courses really depends on you, your academic ability, and the actual time and effort you are willing to dedicate to being successful in that particular class or program. If you decide to take an AP class, enter the IB program, or register for a Dual Enrollment class, you must be sure that you are prepared for the rigor of the coursework including an increase in workload which is going to take a lot more of your time and definitely good time-management skills. Some students may prefer the option of not taking advanced classes and just focus their energy on keeping their GPA as high as possible. Both strategies can work depending on what your trying to achieve. Be aware that a low final grade in an advanced class may actually hurt your GPA rather than raise your GPA. **Challenging yourself academically** is very important, but do not be coerced into taking any of these courses if you are not ready to apply yourself nor have the time to dedicate to the increased workload.

    Not to sound repetitive, but, taking advanced courses in high school "is highly recommended" if you are looking for academic challenges, testing your readiness for college, or want a grade bump to increase your GPA. If you are looking for scholarship opportunities, financial aid, or grants, then higher GPA's, test scores and class rankings are what colleges look for as proof of academic excellence and potential. Be sure to research your desired schools and their qualifications well ahead of time so that you place yourself in a competitive academic position when it is time to submit applications. Colleges want successful students and want you to be successful at their school!

    Let's define the three types of accelerated programs: There could be subtle differences depending on your state, your school district or your high school. Conduct your own research for additional information.

AP courses follow a curriculum mandated by the "College Board". These courses may require prerequisites and "AP exams are required" for college credit. These courses have a higher rigor than traditional general classes and require more reading, in-depth knowledge of the subject matter and an increased workload. The benefit is that the grading system, while harder, uses a different scale. (5.0 scale rather than a 4.0 scale) For example, a B in a AP course is held in higher regard than a B in a general course when applying to colleges; a B in an AP course is counted as an A on your weighted GPA. This calculation may vary in your district so be sure to do your research. Subject tests are required at the end of each course to determine if college credit is received. If you want to take advantage of an AP class, you will want to get the best final grade possible. Taking multiple AP courses per year can be very stressful and time-consuming- be sure that you are up to the task.

Please remember that when applying to colleges, no two colleges will take AP classes and exams into consideration quite the same way. The extent to which colleges will give credit or placement varies among individual colleges as some accept weighted GPA's and other colleges only accept non-weighted GPA's. Doing your homework when researching colleges, their requirements and scores, can make the difference on your acceptance. Entering as a sophomore may impact freshman scholarship opportunities.

IB classes earn a certificate of completion for each class (with a score of 4 or higher), or you can be an IB diploma student, which is a two-year program for juniors and seniors of which preparation your freshmen and sophomore years takes planning. Students who decide to pursue an IB diploma must complete a specific set of courses along with other requirements which your school site can discuss with each student. This type of advanced program is rigorous, time-consuming and comprehensive. You will need to be very dedicated, detailed and focused. Check with your school district for IB programs located near or around your area.

Dual Enrollment classes follow a college curriculum but are taken during high school for college credit. The curriculum is identical to that of the college awarding the credits. There is usually no cost to the student as long as they are a current high school student.

Students that qualify for dual-enrollment classes tend to be high-performing high school students due to the level of rigor involved. Dual enrollment classes require on average about an 8-10 hour increased workload per week over and above your normal school workload and schedule. If you are focused on applying to highly selective universities, or Ivy League schools such as: Harvard, Yale, Dartmouth, etc., be aware that while they may accept your weighted GPA, the class credits are under the discretion of each university. Also, check with your local school district for the advanced programs available.

There is no doubt that these advanced programs and classes can help prep you for the rigors of college, strengthen your transcript and in many cases, give you a head start on college requirements. In some cases, these advanced classes may also help you save tuition money by earning (free) college credit advancing you beyond freshman year.

Please be aware that exceptions to this cost saving plan may vary. If you are looking for freshmen scholarship opportunities and you start college as a sophomore due to credits earned, you may disqualify yourself for certain freshmen scholarship opportunities. Please check with your desired university(s) for accurate information and applicability.

Each student has an unweighted GPA and a weighted GPA depending on any advanced classes they have completed and upon passing the exam(s). An unweighted GPA is the average of all class grades based on a 0 - 4.0 academic scale. A weighted GPA uses a scale of 0 - 5.0, and takes into account accelerated classes which, depending on the grade, have a higher GPA value.

No matter what type of program, class or rigor you decide to undertake, remember it is important to protect your GPA by working hard for your grades if you take accelerated classes. Do not over-commit yourself by taking too many accelerated classes at one time or by over-extending yourself academically. Remember, good time-management skills can be critical for this type of increased work-load. (See Chapter 4, What Is Time Management?)

In regards to college applications, you must do your own homework and research. I would be doing you a disservice by telling you how colleges look at grades and transcripts. Every situation is different and the information continually changes year to year. Students, you must do your own homework by researching the requirements of your desired college(s) as soon as you know a direction you want to go. This responsibility lies fully on your shoulders to investigate. School counselors can also assist you in this important process so reach out to them and definitely plan ahead.

Chapter Four
What Is Time Management?

Time management skills are important for every student to learn so you can manage all the activities and obligations that are part of your daily life now and in your future.

So, what is "time management" in terms of being a student? Time management could be described as a student's ability to "plan the amount of time you spend on each activity". By planning and balancing the amount of time necessary for your academics, extracurricular activities and daily living activities, you will increase your productivity and decrease your stress level. Sound like a good plan?

As a high school student, you will have an increase in homework and assignments than middle school. Your social world will expand and sports, clubs and activities will require more of your time. Maintaining some sort of balance between all of your obligations is important so that you do not get too over-stressed and become unhealthy. An over-emphasis in any one area or areas of your life, or anyone's life, places a stress on the remaining areas. Evaluate your new time needs as a high school student, set your priorities and be sure you have a balance in your life.

How do you see your schedule on a daily basis? Create your own balanced time management chart by listing your activities and the amount of time dedicated to each activity. Identify and list each of your daily demands: academics, sports practice and workouts, extracurricular school activities, family time, social life, alone time, etc. to visualize what your schedule looks like. Try to balance all of your activities while prioritizing those you feel are most important.

Analyze your current time management schedule frequently as you move throughout each grading period. Making changes necessary for success should be a goal of each and every student.

What is Procrastination?

Procrastination is the putting off, by habit or intentionally, those things that should be done. If you are a procrastinator, then you either put off or delay doing something.

By putting your academics off and falling behind, you actually create more stress in your life and may make it more difficult for you to catch up. The many reasons students procrastinate may be due to apathy (you do not care), just plain laziness, or you work better under pressure. Don't make your life more difficult rather than taking care of your business in a timely manner.

If you tend to procrastinate, then you need to evaluate and understand why you do this, learn ways to deal with it or to overcome it. If you can identify and define your distractions, then perhaps you can learn how to avoid it.

Staying on top of your assignments and tests is far easier and less stressful than constantly trying to catch up all the time.

Why Do Student-Athletes Need Time Management Skills?

Athletes, due to the considerable amount of time, effort and commitment required to practice, compete and travel with a team, require more structure and balance in their daily schedules than the typical student. If you are planning on pursuing sports at the college level, you must be focused and dedicated to successfully balancing both your academics and athletics at the high school level. You are called a student-athlete because you are a student first, then an athlete. It would be a mistake and miscalculation on your part to focus more on your athletic demands than your academics. When comparing two athletes with the same athletic abilities, recruiters may also evaluate and compare your academic record.

There are approximately 8 million students currently participating in high school athletics in the United States and only approximately 480,000 spots to compete at NCAA schools (not all full-ride scholarships).

Scholarships are very competitive and academics is often a critical component to any scholarship. Colleges look for athletes that have shown consistent academic effort and progress throughout high school as they are making an investment in you! Place yourself in a great position academically, athletically and in good character so that you shine above others when it is time for signing. Colleges and Universities do not have the money nor are willing to jeopardize their integrity on "high- risk" student-athletes.

Always Prepare a Plan "B"

Choosing a career goal and working toward that goal is excellent planning and could be considered having a "Plan A". But, sometimes "stuff happens" or you just "change your mind" and you regroup, reassess and move on to another plan of action. This alternative path, an acceptable second or third goal choice, could be considered a "Plan B". You may even have many "Plan B's". Having a drive and passion for a particular path is great, but be flexible, investigate all of your options and keep an open mind as you mature, gain experience and exposure to many career paths.

Not all first choices in careers become a reality – so keep your options open and exercise an open mind!

Prepare yourself to be adaptable and resilient. Always be willing to try new career experiences, explore internships and talk to individuals working in your chosen areas of interest. By creating at least one "Plan B", where you have more than one future goal choice for yourself, you will have the ability, interest and motivation to exercise and implement your options if necessary.

For some athletes, having a dream of playing a professional sport, is their "Plan A". Not to say that this cannot become a reality, but the odds are slim due to the competition and low percent of jobs even available. Injuries may also derail your "Plan A". Do not give up the dream, just prepare yourself by having a "Plan B" in case you changed your mind about Plan A, or perhaps your situation changed and it just didn't work out.

Having worked at the University and Olympic levels as a Certified Athletic Trainer, I have witnessed many athletes who have had to change their dream and lifetime goal in athletics due to injury, illness, or an unexpected life event. Some athletes have even chosen to return to college for an advanced degree. This also reiterates the importance and influence that academics can have in your future at any point during your lifetime. You might be surprised as to how many high achieving individuals, including athletes, have utilized their "plan B" and achieved equal or greater success and satisfaction. Nothing is absolutely sure in life and "stuff happens"!

A person who has also learned resilience can better adapt to change and adversity than someone who has poor coping skills.

Straight from the Horse's Mouth

"How to balance out my time and get things done quicker. I have also learned that you should choose your friends carefully because they can be harmful to you, and it happens a lot."

"To never slack off. Even if you think that it's okay not to study or turn in an assignment that will affect your grade either in that moment or in the long run. Balance your social life and your work life. Take school seriously and don't think it is okay to put in half the effort."

"You will have to take charge for your own education and should not expect someone to help you with all of your problems."

"Time really does go by very quickly. Just yesterday it feels like I was a new student that had no idea where to go or what to do in a big school. You can easily pace yourself and know your limits to getting your work done or even paying attention. Sooner or later the year must come to an end and you will end up regretting not getting in work or being able to manage getting your grade higher."

"Don't wait until the last minute; once you fall in a hole, the hole keeps getting deeper, so you better dig yourself out sooner than later."

"To always focus and work hard on your school work and quality over quantity. Education should be your top priority, I also learned that a few close friends is better than a lot of friends/acquaintances."

"Pay attention in class and not to mess around because it did not help me all throughout first semester."

"Never stop trying. Have a good attitude and be optimistic. If you push through with the bare minimum, it won't get you very far; but if you give it your all, you are guaranteed to do good."

"Not to waste time and to pay attention in class. I learned these two lessons in Math class. I had not paid attention to the lesson and I wasted time afterwards trying to figure out how to do the math. After that, I pay attention to all of my lessons and complete any work I get right away."

Chapter Five
Extra-Curricular Activities –
Being Involved Matters!

Whether it is sports, clubs, or leadership activities, they all take time out of your busy schedule. That being said, being involved in high school activities enhances most every student's high school experience and creates a connection to your school and to your peers. These activities will help you expand your social network, assist you in developing good friends that have similar interests/goals and increase your self-confidence. Step out of your comfort zone and take a chance on new experiences, new clubs, and new friends. You might surprise yourself as to how much it enriches your high school life.

Read particularly the senior student reflections in **Straight from the Horse's Mouth** which state that they had missed opportunities to create new friendships and wished that they had taken more time to get more involved in high school activities.

College and University applications that show self-reflection, resiliency, growth in taking initiatives, school involvement, club leadership positions, sports, and community service are usually held in higher regard. Find activities that will set yourself apart from others and challenge yourself to reach "outside the box" for opportunities that encourage both academic and personal growth. Be diversified!

Straight from the Horse's Mouth

"If I could change one thing it would be to participate in more school events. I would try to go to the little things I thought weren't going to be fun or I thought that no one would go with me and I missed so much."

"I would try to enjoy school activities more such as: dances, football games and participate in spirit days."

"Hang around people that have the same interests as you."

"I would have joined more clubs and joined a sports team. I did not think I had enough time, but I could have fit it in."

"The most valuable lesson I could give out to others as I graduate is the fact that being social will get you long ways. Reason being is because coming from my experience, I became more social and more interactive and wanting to meet new people. Those new people I have met changed my life definitely with who I have become as a person and what I strive to do in the future. (EMT)"

Community Service Hours

Most all high schools across the country require community service hours for graduation. Do not underestimate the influence of the accumulation of your community service hours nor the diversity of your experiences on your college applications. Most high schools acknowledge your service hours and some colleges have even been known to award small scholarships for impressive amounts of community service hours. Community service hours may also open doors for job opportunities and create connections within the community.

Tips:

- Start accumulating service hours now during your freshman year. Do not wait until senior year when you are super busy with other obligations.

- Diversify your volunteer experiences.

- Become involved in a leadership role if possible and perhaps even initiate a program, club or activity at school.

- Document all hours on a service log. Make an extra copy or take a picture of your volunteer sheet as you accumulate your hours. This may come in handy if it is lost.

- Create a 4-year template of the events you are involved in starting your freshman through senior years. Instructions are found in the next segment detailing how to set it up and the importance of keeping it updated.

Create Your Own 4-Year High School Template

I highly recommend that each and every high school student, regardless of what path you think you may follow after high school, create your own resume template as early as the beginning of your freshmen year. This "footprint" is a running activity log in a word or google document consisting of all of your activities, awards, grades, community service, and reflection comments over the next four years. This collated information will help to ensure that you do not forget important information, accolades and experiences when it is time to fill out required college or job applications. It is much easier to create this document in the beginning of freshman year than to have to re-create all of your activities, dates and leadership positions 3 ½ years later.

Date	Year	Activity	Description	Sponsor
10/12/18	9th	Water Polo	Most improved award	H.S. Club
8/2018-5/2021	9, 10, 11, 12	Club Water Polo	Player	H.S. Club
12/10/2019	11, 12	Debate	Captain 12th	H.S. Club
9/6/19-6/6/21	10, 11, 12	Sports-Medicine	Officer 11th, 12th	H.S. Club Athletic Training
9/6/20	9th	Community Service	Booth monitoring	Elementary Fair

Now, take the time to create your 4-year template detailing your own high school footprint!

Chapter Six
Academic Challenges

Students, at the high school level, the task of monitoring your own grades is your job. Some of you have been successfully performing this task in middle school, so the transition of monitoring your grades in high school should be very similar. If you are a student who has not really paid attention to your grades, then now is the time for you to start being responsible for your actions and efforts and take control of your grades, assignments, tests and homework. Set up your school portal and begin today.

If you are a student-athlete involved in school athletics, there is usually some type of grade-check method used by coaches in-season to verify your eligibility compliance. If you are struggling academically, then you need to understand that more of your time and effort needs to be dedicated to your academics. If you fail a class or two, then you may jeopardize your sports eligibility and you will have to re-arrange your schedule to retake each class for credit recovery.

There is no doubt that freshman year is often an experiment in time-management, establishing priorities and balancing a social life. But, make no mistake, academics do count freshman year and as a student, starting off with strong grades should be your goal.

Create a calendar and time management system which includes your homework assignments, studying time and athletic activities so that you are successful in balancing all of the commitments in your life.

Motivating some students where consequences are tied to effort and outcome can be very effective.

Parents, if your student chooses not to be accountable for their own grades, tends to procrastinate or has a prior history of incomplete or missing work, then he/she would benefit from your implementing a grade monitoring system either on a weekly, bimonthly or monthly basis. Begin freshman year by having your student print out their grades from their student portal for you to see and review with them. It is not enough for you to see their grades on a parent portal, it is about them being accountable to printing out their own grades, reviewing the scores with a parent, and explaining and adjusting the effort needed for their success. This method has proven to have a profound, positive effect on a student's effort, particularly if it is tied to consequences such as: phone usage, computer time, social time, free time.

Most schools have an online student information system which includes student and parent portals. Both the student and the parent receive a portal login for access to grade reports, scores on assignments, tests, quizzes, missing assignments, or late assignments. As your student shows consistency or improvement, weekly monitoring reports can be reduced to bi-monthly or monthly as the desired grade outcome is reached. Struggling students that are academically accountable to a parent or mentor appear more motivated than those that are unaccountable to anyone.

Straight from the Horse's Mouth

"I wish I took school more seriously in the beginning. Because I knew I hated school, it took a toll on my grades so I limited myself and projected an image that made me look a lot less intelligent than I really am."

"For me to focus more first semester. I should have paid more attention in class and done my work. My grades were better second semester because I paid attention and did my work."

"The most valuable lesson that I have learned in my four years is to always try. No matter how hard the class material is, or no matter how hard the teacher grades, you CANNOT get frustrated and pull away from the material and give up on the class. Make the deadlines. Do the homework. Pay attention. Just try. School is not hard unless you make it that way for yourself."

Academic Success Plans (SST, IEP, 504 Plan)

Academic success plans may vary state by state, but take the time to research information that can apply to your particular area and/or situation.

Parent Support is Critical for Your Student's Success

Academic success plans are very specific to each student who qualifies and identifying a learning disability is the first step in helping a student to become successful in learning. The laws are very specific, but may have some differences state to state. For an individualized educational plan (IEP), a student needs to be identified, assessed, and qualify prior to its development and implementation. There are also accommodation plans and assistive plans for students at all levels. General information on the more common academic assistive plans are identified below and contact with your school counselors is advised for more specific or detailed information.

SST - Student Study Team

An SST or a "Student Study Team" is designed to support students that are having difficulty in the regular classroom. Student's that can benefit from such a meeting is one that is not progressing academically, a student that is struggling with their behavior in class, a student that is not interested in applying themselves nor engaging in class. This SST meeting can be initiated by either the student's teacher, parent or administrator. An SST team (teacher, counselor, administrator and parent) is then formed to further examine a student's academic, behavioral and social-emotional progress.

As opposed to a parent-teacher conference, which focuses on improving communication and addressing specific class problems, an SST meeting provides teachers, administrators, the student and their parent, with an opportunity to share concerns regarding this student and to develop a plan for student success. The interventions agreed upon will vary depending on the student's educational needs with a common goal of assisting the student to achieve academic success.

504 Plan- Learning or Attention Issues, Injury or Illness Accommodation

The "504" in a 504 plan" refers to Section 504 of the Rehabilitation Act and the Americans with Disabilities Act. This is a plan that provides services and changes to the student's learning environment to meet the needs of the student. There are two requirements to qualify for a 504 plan. First, the student must have a diagnosed learning or attention issue sometimes contributed to by an injury or illness. Second, the disability must interfere with the student's ability to learn in a general education classroom.

The 504 plan usually begins with the parent obtaining a letter from their doctor or other medical professional stating your student's diagnosis and taking it to the counseling office. The counselor will then begin the process of developing a plan with the student, parent and an administrator. Examples of diagnoses that may utilize this plan may be in the case of a concussion, car accident or sudden illness where time, rest and education modifications are critical to a student's recovery.

Individualized Educational Plan – IEP

If your student receives special education services, they will have an Individualized Educational Plan (IEP), which is a plan or program that identifies your student's learning needs, the services the school will provide and how progress will be measured. Several people will be involved in creating this document- parents, student, counselors, teachers and administrators. This process is an effective way to identify your student's strengths and weaknesses and to create a plan for student success in school.

It is vital for any student's academic success plan that the parent(s) attend these meetings and the student engage in the process. Creating a plan is easy, but the follow through by both the student and parent is critical to its success. All of this being said, it is important to understand that the student's ultimate success lies on them, their effort and engagement.

STUDENTS AND PARENTS – Why Do Some Students Get Failing Grades?

There are an infinite number of reasons or combination of reasons why a student fails a class (or two). Poor study habits, lack of motivation, inadequate preparation to be successful, lack of self-esteem or confidence which prevents students from building on their strengths, and little or no interest or motivation in pursuing their academics. These are just a few contributory reasons why some students are not successful in school. A more detailed list will follow on the next page.

Struggling students may have been able to survive elementary and middle school with minimal effort and focus, only to find out that in high school, the same level effort and focus results in failing a class or two or three.

In many school districts, failing one or more classes in middle school does not necessarily keep you from progressing to the next grade level whereas failing a class in high school can impact your ability to graduate with a high school diploma. A high school diploma requires that you earn a designated amount of credits to graduate. If you become too deficient in credits to graduate, you may be required to take additional classes for credit recovery or move to an alternative school.

A high school diploma or GED is the minimal standard required by most entry level jobs, entering the military, as well as application to colleges and universities.

Excuses for failing classes that I have heard over the years include:

- Student does not have an interest in learning- doing work and or homework (this could be a continuing problem since elementary school and/or middle school).

- Student complains it is too hard to keep up or the work is too hard.

- Student has not developed any type of learning structure outside the classroom including a homework routine.

- Student feels too behind in work assignments to ever catch up in a class and therefore give up.

- Student believes that their parents do not value or take an interest in their academics - why should they?

- Student is below proficiency level in a certain subject and cannot envision themselves catching up and being successful.

- Student believes they are going to get a sports scholarship and do not have to worry so much about their academics.

- Student is at school solely for the social aspect.

- Student has no accountability or consequences at home for their time or grades.

- Student has never felt what success feels like.

- Student is simply not motivated to do anything.

- Student is more interested in friendships than academics and sacrifice their academic achievement for acceptance by friends.

- Student lacks a positive mentor that can inspire good values and a solid work ethic.

- Student has associated themselves with the wrong group of kids that are unmotivated and make poor choices (Example: drugs and/or alcohol).

- Student does not have a vision for their future or cannot see life choices beyond high school.

A student that does not have a purpose or vision for their future seems to struggle the most. Despite "the village approach" where many individuals try to help a single student and implement academic success plans, if the student does not make the effort and cares less than the village, then success is more unlikely. How do we encourage a student to care?

Unfortunately, we do not have a crystal ball to determine the perfect answers to motivate these struggling students, but I do believe that promoting self-worth and self-esteem is a significant factor for their eventual success. Whatever the reason(s) are, we as an educational system still need to keep searching and seek for the answers so that we may help these struggling students become successful, functional, and contributing members in society.

Student's Behavior in the Classroom

Students, have you displayed past behavior issues in elementary and/or middle school for the purpose of popularity and/or attention? If so, you will find your behavior quite unpopular at the high school level. The student population is older, maturity levels have risen, students are investing themselves more in class, and your peers are emotionally moving on with or without you.

Understand that teachers have only a set number of minutes each period to teach a concept, practice a concept, reteach it again if necessary and then test the concept. Some of your classes will consist of students of all ages and grades, all learning styles and focus abilities which makes the classroom time extremely important. Teachers want to teach; they do not want to take valuable class time to constantly discipline or re-direct students whose main interest is to distract other students or to bide their own time until the bell rings. Continued behavior issues or class disruptions can be subject to school disciplinary actions followed by behavioral success plans.

Although there are an infinite number of reasons for the lack of success of some students, as mentioned above, there is no reason for a student to disrupt an entire class because they feel like it or they are bored. At the end of the day, it all comes down to the student's choices.

There is no doubt that some parents do all of the right things but still have students that rebel, have a lack of interest in school, and/or act out in the classroom. An intervention that may address this issue is "shadowing". School counselors are very knowledgeable in this arena and should be your first resource if pursuing this intervention is necessary.

Parents
What is "shadowing"?

Parents, "shadowing" your student at school can be an option as a corrective intervention for student behavior in the classroom.

Shadowing your student involves the parent attending school along side their student and following in their footsteps by attending each class together. Observing your student's interactions, behavior and focus in the classroom is the goal even though they may be on their best behavior for that day.

There is no doubt that it is inconvenient for a parent to take the time or day off of work, but the outcome will hopefully be worthwhile. Your student certainly does not want their parent following them around on campus every day. Proving that your student can behave in the classroom is important, otherwise, scheduling an SST and creating a behavior plan would be the next step. This intervention is usually arranged through the counselors' office or administration office. Shadowing, in some cases, is also used as an alternative to suspension in some school districts. Understandably, most students do not want their parent(s) following them around at school. Shadowing only one time may be enough to make the positive changes you are looking for in your student's behavior. Check with your high school counselors or administration to determine if this practice or other similar alternative programs may exist at your school which may offer you similar results.

Be Consistent and Follow-Through with Consequences

Consistency and follow-through are very important qualities for parents to continue to practice and demonstrate through the high school years.

As parents, setting deadlines, consequences and following-through may be much easier to control at the work setting where your environment is more controlled than in our own homes. In many homes, there are many more moving pieces which may make the setting of guidelines and establishing consequences more difficult. The actual follow-through may be hit or miss which often results in a poor outcome for behavior change. If the follow-through seldom or rarely happens, then students know there is no consequence; if there is no consequence, then there is little or no need to change behavior.

Students are well aware whether their parent(s) will follow-through or not; we have proved it to them over and over, right? As a parent, I am just as guilty as anyone. But, we will not see a change in our student's behavior unless they see, believe, and experience our follow-through on a consequence. "Say what you mean" and "mean what you say". While students may not like the consequences, they will respect your ability to follow-through and can adapt. There is no doubt it takes much more time and effort, but hopefully your objective of better grades and/or positive behavior changes will be rewarded.

Student Advocate

Chapter Seven
The Many Roles of a High School Counselor?

A high school counselor is an integral and vital member of your educational team. Their role has expanded over the years, but their constant mission is to be an advocate for the well-being of all students. Some of their many roles include: steering students toward academic achievement, career counseling, social/emotional development, overseeing accommodation plans, triaging emotional, mental and behavioral issues, conflict mediation, and class selections.

In some schools across the country, the number of counselors has unfortunately decreased even though their job description and workload has increased. Some counseling offices have expanded to a more comprehensive team approach which also includes: psychologists, social workers, and specialists to meet the growing and ever changing needs of today's students.

While mental health issues have always plagued this age group, the increased rate at which these issues are surfacing have indicated a far greater need for schools to seek out and provide additional services to meet today's student population.

Mental Health of Students – a growing concern!

"A U.S. Surgeon General report indicates that one in five children and adolescents will face a significant mental health condition during their school years. Up to one in five kids living in the U.S. shows signs or symptoms of a mental health disorder in a given year. So, in a school classroom of 25 students, five of them may be struggling with the same issues many adults deal with: depression, anxiety, substance abuse."
nassp.org/advocacy

The statistics are real, the impact on our youth is staggering. Students with mental health issues need to be heard, identified, offered resources and surrounded by a support system. Some of the problems that schools are facing today can be tied to those struggling students experiencing, and in some cases, suffering from mental health issues. Chronic absences, failing of classes leading to a high number of drop-outs and/or behavior issues are just a few areas that schools are trying to address. Identifying and tackling these issues are increasingly more difficult as the numbers continue to increase with too little access or assistance.

If you are a student who struggles with any type of mental health issue, please take advantage of your counseling department services at your school. There is help available for you! Never be afraid to ask for help!

If you have a friend or an acquaintance that exhibits signs of a life-threatening mental condition, or someone who appears that they may harm themselves or others, do not waste time contemplating whether or not to seek help. Report their behavior as soon as possible to an adult, to your teachers, counselors or to an administrator.

Do not take any life-threatening situation on yourself as it "is bigger than you" and takes a mental health professional to provide the care necessary.

Teaching high school Health class was very impactful for my students and it created many teachable moments. The awareness of mental health issues, coping skills, resilience and numerous other health topics were relatable to many as they were suffering silently or knew friends that were struggling. Learning about the signs, symptoms and triggers for various conditions and illness are life-long skills that students can take with them into adulthood. Current topics such as: eating disorders, depression, stages of grief, drugs and alcohol, and STD's created a lot of thought-provoking conversations. Health Education teaches students skills they will use throughout their lifetime.

Learning about health motivates students to create a healthy lifestyle, understand the disease process and reduce risky behaviors. Unfortunately, Health Education is only a graduation requirement in selected states or school districts. By requiring Health class and including CPR certification as a graduation requirement around the country, we could empower our youth with knowledge and life-skills that they will carry with them throughout their lifetime. Who knows, they might even save a life or two...or three...

Real Life Story

An example of how friends can help friends and the value of advocating for your friends was evident in a classroom situation of mine a few years ago. I had just taught a health lesson on the signs and symptoms of depression and suicidal red flag behaviors. At the end of class, a student approached me regarding a friend that exhibited similar red flag behaviors. I referred the concerned student to a counselor so that she could share her observations about her friend. The counselor provided a rapid response by conducting a "wellness check" of the student at lunchtime.

During that discussion, the student admitted to the counselor that he was struggling emotionally and had planned to commit suicide that very afternoon after school. This student was very fortunate that he had a friend who listened to him and was concerned enough to seek help on his behalf and advocate for his well-being. Also recognized is the counselor for her quick response to the needs of her students, identifying his condition and securing him the help necessary to keep him safe.

That concerned student, by going to the counselor's office out of concern for her friend, just saved her friend's life. This is how empowering knowledge and caring about your fellow peers can be.

Experience in addressing this type of mental health crisis requires specific training that students and most teachers do not have. Counselors have both the education and the experience in this area to provide students the help or to make referrals for them if necessary.

I have always told my students that "I would rather lose a friendship (by telling an adult) than I would lose a friend".

Be a strong advocate for yourself and for your friends if they are unable to do it for themselves.

College Guidance

Another reason students should value your high school counselors and get to know them is because they will help guide you academically through your four years of high school, help you with class selection each year and assist you in navigating through the college process. Counselors know the "ins and outs" regarding college/university requirements and the application process. They want you to be successful and can help prepare you for the direction you choose leading up to graduation.

If your chosen path is college, placing yourself in a competitive position prior to application time is extremely important. Completing college applications and financial forms can be very confusing, tedious and lengthy, so be sure to schedule an appointment with your counselor well before the deadline so that they can give you the best possible attention at guiding you through this exciting process. Most high school counseling departments offer parent/student nights dealing with the college application process. This is a great opportunity to receive accurate information about the college application process making your transition much easier and less stressful. Take advantage of seminars offered through your counseling department. It is well worth your time!

Recommendations are also an important part of the application process. It is important when choosing teachers, counselors, administrators, or employers for references that they actually know you, your academic record, character, work ethic and your career goals. Reference letters take time to write as they are very individualized and some of your mentors may be asked to write several in a short period of time in addition to their normal workload. Requesting recommendations well ahead of time is important as well as making sure you have built and established a relationship with them over the past 2-4 years. Please be considerate of their time for all those supporting you in this exciting process.

College Options: The Differences Between a Junior (Community) College and a 4-Year College and a University

Junior Colleges may also be referred to as a **Community Colleges** in some areas of the country. These are generally public schools that offer 2-year Associate's degrees, diplomas and certificates. Community Colleges are designed for students who want to complete their prerequisites prior to a four-year college, those who want vocational training or different career options.

Students usually commute from home or reside in nearby housing. Working full or part time while taking classes is also common. The cost of a 2-year Community College is quite a bit lower than the cost of a 4-year College or University which makes it a good financial decision if this is your priority. Be aware of how impacted these schools are in your area if you have a time deadline to complete your coursework. In some cases, course selection can be limited or not offered each grading period, delaying your transfer or graduation timeline.

A **College** is referred to as a smaller educational institution that offers undergraduate (four-year degrees) and associates (two-year degrees) in some cases. College life is uniquely smaller than a University and more comfortable to some looking for a lower student population. Campus life is an integral part of the atmosphere. Students reside in on-campus and off-campus housing and enjoy the "college experience".

A **University** is referred to as a larger educational institution that offers four-year Undergraduate, a Master's - advanced graduate degrees, and/or Ph.D. degrees. Some Universities also have attached Law, Medical, or

Veterinary Schools for those wanting to pursue a professional degree. Course offerings are more diverse and include a greater number of programs as compared to a College. A University campus life is an integral part of the atmosphere and students reside either on-campus or in nearby housing.

Throughout the country, the differences within each educational institution are numerous, so do your research and find that special place that excites you to learn and meets your needs. Aside from the educational value, factors you may want to consider will be: tuition cost (Junior or Community College being the lowest), living expenses (on campus and off campus), private or public college, in-state or out-of-state tuition, climate, cost-of-living in that particular area of the country which may affect housing rates off campus, graduation rate, support systems available and safety. There are numerous other factors you may want to consider that are more personal to your situation.

For students that reside in the WICHE Region, take a look at qualifying for the **WUE "woo-wee"**, Western Undergraduate Exchange program which is a regional tuition-reciprocity agreement. States that are included in this agreement are: Alaska, Arizona, California, Colorado, Hawai'i, Idaho, Montana, Nevada, New Mexico, North Dakota, Oregon, South Dakota, U.S. Pacific Territories and Freely Associated States, Utah,

Washington and Wyoming. If awarded, out-of-state tuition is significantly decreased making it more affordable. In some cases, the WUE out-of-state tuition is lower than some in-state tuition schools. To qualify for the WUE, check the educational institution(s) you are applying to in order to determine your eligibility. Many schools use a student's major, GPA, and ACT or SAT scores as criteria. Again, no two schools are the same - do your homework!

Keep in mind the following when looking at your educational choices after high school:

Your typical two-year Junior or Community College may extend your time to three+ years before transferring if you cannot get the classes you need. Be aware of impacted schools where it may be difficult to schedule sequenced or required classes due to too many students and not enough teachers or class offerings. Remember, most Colleges and Universities require you to complete all of your two-year pre-requisites before being eligible to transfer to a four-year educational institution.

Also be aware of your in-state four-year Colleges and Universities if they happen to be impacted, limiting your class selection as it may take you five plus years to graduate instead of the average four years. This delay may extend your tuition and living expenses which can accumulate well beyond that of a four-year out-of-state tuition expense.

Be sure to research the cost of living in the area of your chosen institution as you will most likely spend only one or two years in the dorm and then live off-campus. In some areas of the country, the cost of living expenses can exceed the tuition costs. Also, conversely, some areas that are less expensive to live can offset the tuition costs even if they are out-of-state.

Take the time to research each school you are interested in attending and compare: the academics, the geographical area, the demographics, the weather, the cost of living, ... so that you make the right decision for the right reasons.

Be sure to research all financial scholarship opportunities such as: active or retired military, academic scholarships, college presidential scholarships, community service scholarships, etc.

Research alternative career paths such as: the military, trade-school, work sector, etc. There is a path for everyone, so reach out and know that you may change your mind and major once or twice until you find what is a right fit for you. Have a "Plan A" and at least one "Plan B".

Better to try something and change your mind, then it is to never try and miss an opportunity.

Straight from the Horse's Mouth

"Research career options so that I could select courses more focused on my choice(s). Course exposure in those fields could help me in college courses."

"One lesson I learned and pass onto incoming freshman, is that high school will make you feel like it's every man for himself. You are going to lose a lot of friends, and people are busy with their own lives so you need to learn how to be your own support system, your own advocate, and be your own rock. Everyone's going to get into your business so you have to learn how to keep some things to yourself or else everyone will find out."

"Don't hold yourself back from doing things. I feel like we get so caught up in our school work, that we allow it to take away from our time we have as kids. Our time in high school is very limited due to college. So, try not to let yourself or others hold you back. Enjoy the time you have with your friends, and don't stress about the little things in life."

"As a senior, I have learned that it is important to communicate to those around you. Communication is not only talking, but also listening. Students should understand that their counselors have helped many students with various problems, their teachers are well-educated and versed in their subjects, and many of their peers are always willing to help one another out. With this being said, younger students should not be afraid to ask questions or ask for help; they should always be willing to listen."

"Throughout my senior year, I have experienced and seen many forms of expressions. Stress, excitement, focus, and sadness were the primary things I have felt. Stress for those who don't know what they want to do after high school or they are afraid they won't graduate. Excitement to leave high school and enter the real world. Focus to make sure they pass and get ready for college, and sadness for those who know they will never experience this event again in their lives."

"Don't hold yourself back from doing things. I feel like we get caught up in our school work, that we allow it to take away from our time we have as kids. Enjoy the time you have with your friends, and don't stress about the little things in life."

"I feel that vibes change as each student goes through the four years of high school. Freshman year they start off nervous, drama obsessed, and uptight. Sophomore year they slowly start to break out of their comfort shell, and by Junior year, they become more focused on getting good grades because they have to start thinking about the colleges they want to get into. Lastly, by senior year I feel like we become more relaxed, and stress less."

"The most important thing I learned over the year is that procrastination is always joked about but it truly will kill your grades, sleep and stress levels. If you have work that is due in a week, do it the day you get it so you have the rest of the week to relax instead of the day before. Early done work is good and you can make sure to go back and make it perfect. Rushed work is not great work."

"Senior year is a little of everything; excited to graduate, nervous to be an adult, senioritis, scared and maybe depressed."

"Stay on task. Try to balance things out between having fun and getting your education. If you work hard now, you will be thanking yourself in the long run."

Chapter Eight
Is College the Right Choice for Every Student After High School?

The assumption that every graduating senior wants to continue on to a college immediately after high school is FALSE. Time, money, passion and access are some factors that students consider when making their choices.

The chosen paths of graduating seniors are very diverse, but their concerns year after year remain very similar:

- I want to play a sport in a Division I or Division II school.

- I want to go into the military first, then military will pay my college costs.

- I need to get a job first, then I will think of college.

- College is not for me right now.

- I don't really like school enough right now to continue my education. Maybe later.

- College is on my radar, but not sure where. I want to go to a Community College first to save money, then transfer to a four-year University.

- I want to attend college, then join the military as an officer.

- I cannot afford to go to college right now so I will work for a year.

- I am not sure what I want to do yet so I do not want to waste my money on going to college.

- I want to travel the world first, then consider going.

- I want to go to a large University and experience it all.

- I want to pursue a trade instead.

- I think I want to go into the police force or fire academy.

- I want to become an EMT and paramedic.

- I want to become a pilot.

There are numerous other thoughts and paths that students pursue and there are no right or wrong answers. **The correct choice is the one you make as it is your life to live.**

Choosing a Trade or Job-Ready Career CTE – Career Technical Education

In many high schools across the country, there has been an emergence of CTE, or Career Technical Education classes. Some schools have been on the cutting edge of CTE for several years and some high schools are just formulating their pathways. Attitudes are shifting from education that requires only degrees or advanced degrees to innovative job-ready career options. These choices are more hands-on, flexible, dual-training consisting of part time on-the-job training mixed with part time classroom education leading to internships, apprenticeships, certificates, licenses and job-ready careers.

Career Technical Education encourages students to explore career options and prepare for an occupation in a selected industry or career sector. A CTE program offers courses in a multi-year sequence and integrates core academic knowledge with an internship that offers technical and occupational experience leading to certifications, careers or continued education upon graduation. CTE programs give you a hands-on experience and insight to help you decide what career options are best suited to your passion(s), talents and knowledge.

CTE Pathways:

1. Cohort Fashion and Interior Design Education

2. Child Development and Family Services

3. Health Science and Medical Technology

4. Hospitality Tourism and Recreation

5. Agriculture and Natural Resources Marketing Sales and Services

6. Business and Finance

7. Arts, Media and Entertainment

8. Public Services Information and Communication Technology

9. Energy, Environment, and Utilities Manufacturing and Product Development

10. Engineering and Architecture Building Construction Trades

11. Transportation

Not all pathways are available at each high school site that provides CTE classes. I encourage all students to investigate what your high school has to offer. The academic knowledge, the experience of an internship, and the exposure to many career choices can make a difference when evaluating your future goals.

What are Employers Looking for in Future Employees?

No matter what your path or education level you have acquired, employers are looking for:

- employees that have the required job skills
- employees that have good communication skills
- employees that have a good work ethic
- employees that are on-time
- employees that are honest
- employees that show good character
- employees that exhibit leadership qualities
- employees that can work independently
- employees that are problem-solvers
- employees that don't create a lot of drama
- employees that want the job and want to work

Can furthering your education increase your earning potential? Yes, certainly in many situations education level is tied to promotions and salary increases. But, your experience is also a valuable asset. Education is knowledge and knowledge and experience together is power.

That being said, there are plenty of self-made successful men and women who believed in themselves and were willing to put in an amazing amount of hard work and dedication to become successful without a college education. Do what is right for you. Don't look back and say- "would've, could've or should've". Pursue your passion, realize your dreams and create your own future.

Chapter 9
Teacher Contact- Students, Be Your Own Advocate!

Students, I have received numerous calls and emails over the years from high school parent(s) such as yours regarding grades. This in itself is not a problem, but if you are to advocate for yourself, then you should make the first contact with your teacher, not your parent. This first contact should be done preferably in person before or after class, with a follow-up email to your teacher. Most teachers will make it clear in the beginning of each grading period as to how they would like to be approached or contacted. If after talking with your teacher, you are not satisfied or do not get a resolution to your situation, then it is reasonable to involve a counselor, parent, and/or request a meeting with all involved.

Communicating "face-to-face" with your teacher(s) is an important skill that will benefit you throughout your lifetime in many types of situations and future jobs. Each teacher is different and has their own personality not unlike students or future bosses. In this particular situation, some teachers may be more approachable than others, but, that will happen in every facet of your life. Figure it out for yourself, develop a relationship with your teacher and communication will be easier. Reach out to your teachers first, then to other sources if necessary, but not until you have given it a good try first!

If trying to communicate face to face with your teacher is not productive or seems very difficult, then I suggest you email your teacher detailing your questions and/or concerns. This email will hopefully provide you with a resolution. If not, then your next step may be to schedule a meeting with your teacher and a parent or counselor. There is a right way of finding a resolution- be your own advocate first, and then utilize other resources if necessary.

On occasion, I have had students ask their parent(s) to intercede on their behalf regarding their grade or about retaking a test. I have also had parents take the initiative to contact a teacher not because you asked them, just based on a conversation you had with your parent regarding a grade.

Students, it is very important to include "all" of the information when discussing questionable grades. Do not place your parent(s) in an awkward situation when they talk with your teacher and you left out "part of the truth". If this occurs, then the parent-teacher call, often a fact-finding mission on the parent's part, results in a plethora of new information for the parent regarding your work effort, classroom behavior, upcoming assignments, missing assignments or test results which may require from you a more detailed explanation to your parent later that night. While this conversation can be productive, it would be far better for you to advocate for yourself; you know the work, the assignment(s) and are creating a working relationship with your teacher.

💡 ***Build relationships with your teachers, shoulder the responsibility for your own actions and your grades - be your own advocate.***

Parents, while raising elementary and middle school students may have had their ups and downs, the control was solidly with the parent. In high school, the academic challenges mixed with hormones and impending adulthood tips the scale of control making it necessary by the parents and students alike to work together to create a "**new normal**" in regards to responsibility, independence and accountability. Teaching our students to be independent and advocate for themselves is a vital part of growing up and a skill that all students need to learn.

If your student comes to you regarding a class or individual test grade concern that they do not understand, then encourage them to discuss it with their teacher first. If they say that they have without resolution, then I suggest to have them follow-up with an email to the teacher reiterating their encounter. (This is mentioned in the student section) This will provide documentation for your student that they have tried to communicate with the teacher and can use this documentation to pursue further resolution. Parent intervention should only be necessary if all other means have been exhausted. Mentoring your students to advocate for themselves is an important life-skill that they will practice and use throughout their lifetime.

Teaching our students to advocate for themselves, requiring accountability of grades and behavior, and responsible time-management is now the "new normal". Mistakes will be made and hopefully lessons will be learned. High School, along with education, is like a training ground for our student's process of maturing into adulthood. Their future goals are closer to reality and their engagement and success in the process will be evidence of their readiness to move on.

Chapter 10
Technology

In today's environment, utilizing computerized technology is second nature at all grade levels and is often used in many classrooms on a daily basis.

Technology also affects almost every facet of our lives today, parents and students alike. Being a responsible user is the key to balancing technology in our home, school, social and personal lives. Keeping students in the real world with actual face-to-face relationships, good personal communication skills and being independent of social media sites is critical for their healthy growth personally as well as professionally in their later life.

Phone usage at school and in the classroom, is usually dictated by your school and district policies. In many schools, phones are allowed under the discretion of the teacher whereas other schools have stricter guidelines that restrict them altogether during school hours. Remember, there is a time and a place where it is applicable and a time and a place where it can be disruptive. District policies are stated on their website and an individual teacher's phone policy is usually posted on their personal school website.

Students

Review all of your teacher's websites at the beginning of each grading period regarding phone use and respect their rules and behavior expectations. Do not be distracted or distract your peer's learning time in the classroom by your phone use. Respect everyone's desire to learn. If you have a phone need that contradicts your teacher's policy, be sure to communicate your need with your teacher prior to class.

The Power of Social Media

Social media can have a powerful impact on many areas of your life including college admissions and obtaining a future job. In some instances, where there may be a red flag on your college application, college admissions may vet a student which will include their social networking sites. Every post you make stays with you, is permanent, can follow you, and is available for anyone to see. Use your common sense, be sure to check your words, be positive, avoid inappropriate photos, cyber-bullying, friending people you do not know or trust, and protect your private information like your social security information, address and phone number.

Your social media sites and postings are a reflection of your character and values. *Be proud of your electronic footprint* and do not place yourself in a vulnerable position where you have to look over your shoulder waiting for someone to reveal a poor decision you may have made at a vulnerable or immature time in your life.

Straight from the Horse's Mouth

"Phones are not the problem, it is the constant need for attention due to social media and messaging. People are too worried about what people think rather than focusing on the important thing... SCHOOL; Yes, phones are extremely distracting."

"Phones can be a positive or negative. I know many students who have used social media to hurt someone they are jealous of. Your school can track the source and then you get into a lot of trouble. My freshman year was worse on social media, but it got better when kids were getting caught. Don't be hurtful!"

"I think phones are distracting to students but I also think that it can be a tool for learning or finding out new things. I think it would be hard to not have my phone for a day or two because it is a means of communication for me and my loved ones. I do think that phones are interrupting my ability to focus on school because anytime I hear my phone buzz, I want to look at who is on the notification."

"Phones can get very distracting sadly. Honestly, I don't know if I could go without my phone in my classes. I have just gotten accustomed to always having it and checking it every so often. Earphones personally help me focus but can also help me to block out lectures when I don't want to listen which is a negative."

"The impact of having phones in the classroom either disrupts or continues the ability of people to work; some students will not put their phones away regardless."

"Phones in the classroom has become a HUGE issue. Many kids are glued to it therefore not listening and unable to set it down. Distraction and frustration can affect teachers and students alike."

"Technology is so convenient now. I have had to clean up my social media sites when I started to apply to colleges and hoped they did not see my previous posts. I wish I had thought or known about it freshman year."

Parents

A hot topic in most households today is phone privacy. I am sure that most students feel protective of their phones and that their phone is private, sacred and a "lifeline" to their world. As a parent, it is certainly your decision as to how private your student's phones actually are, especially if you are paying the bills. Occasionally taking a look at your student's phone will give you a snapshot of what is going on in your student's life. But, beware, some phones are like opening Pandora's box!

There are many phone apps that appear harmless, for example like a calculator. Some apps can also be an undisguisable social media website or worse. Be aware of what is happening in the cyber world and take an interest in what high school students are tuned into.

Technology in the cyber world, although helpful in many ways, can also be very tricky, complicated and deceiving. Unfortunately, most students are usually aware of many of these tricks and deceptions.

If you have any concerns about your student's phone use or misuse, then placing a parent control app on your child's phone dictating when or how much time they can spend on texting, web browsing, or social media sites is available. These parent control apps are also able to provide location tracking, time restrictions, web filtering,

... and the list goes on. If this is of interest to you, research "parent control app", select one that works best for your situation and download the app on both phones. Next, you can literally select the times to turn on/off each individual app. For example, it would be a great idea to turn off the texting app during class times, but yet you can leave on the web app for classroom research and the phone app for emergencies.

You can block texting or social media sites during designated times also using the "parent control apps". Most of these websites also notify parents when they are being tampered with by the user (your student). Parent control apps such as: Our Pact, Bark, Circle, and Teen Safe, are available but do your homework as there are numerous apps available and they all have different costs and features.

Chapter 11
In ALL Relationships...
Character Counts

"Opposites may attract when it comes to personality, but opposites never attract when it comes to character... You are going to get exactly as you are...."
                       Quoted by Pam Stenzel

Students

This is a very profound statement about relationships and one you should at least consider as you start high school. Your friendships will mature, some will dissolve and new friendships will emerge. The choices you will be making in the next four years of high school will mold and reflect your character. You will be establishing more permanent relationships with peers, friends, significant others, teachers, counselors and possibly even in the workplace.

As you move through each year of high school, you may notice some students making poor choices time to time which can be part of their learning curve as a young adult. But, when making choices, you jeopardize someone's character or safety or that of others around you, then it can have a profound effect on your reputation, trustworthiness, and perhaps even your own future. Poor choices may include, but are not be limited to: lying, cheating on tests, asking to copy other's work, shoplifting, stealing, using/selling drugs or alcohol, unprotected sex or other similar risky behaviors.

Character is the most important quality you have that does not cost you to have and can be your most valuable asset now and in your future. Remember, your behavior and your choices dictate your character. If you have damaged your character and reputation, it may take a lot of time and hard work to rebuild other's trust in you. Taking responsibility is the "first step".

No one can take your character away, only YOU can give it away through your actions and words!

Stay Clear of Drama and Bullying

Drama usually revolves around gossip, jealousy and insecurity. Drama is often negative, destructive to relationships, and a drain on your emotions and time. That being said, does this description of drama describe the types of drama you or your friends have seen or been involved in recently?

Focus on what is really important and positive in your life. I do not know many high-schoolers that truly have the time to deal with drama on a daily basis. But, time and time again, students get sucked into other student's drama no matter if it involves them or not. It is understandable that you want to support your friends, but be smart and evaluate the situation thoroughly. If the drama does not directly involve you, step away. You will have measurably more friends and improved quality time in your social relationships by not taking on "other student's battles".

That brings me to the topic of relationships and bullying! Is bullying considered destructive behavior? YES! Is bullying hurtful to others? YES! Is bullying ever positive? NO! Can bullying have life-long effects on some people? YES! Has bullying led some victim(s) to engage in personal destructive behaviors? YES!

From what I have observed at all ages and at all school levels - where there is drama, there is usually some level of bullying and vice versa. If more students would build their friends up instead of tearing them down; if students would understand the hurtfulness they can create on others; if students would treat others the way they would like to be treated; ... then bullying could be greatly reduced or eliminated in our schools and students would be a lot happier.

Students, do not be a part of making someone's life miserable; it is cruel, unfair and mean behavior. Seek help from your high school counselors if you are a victim of bullying or are unable to deal with the emotions associated with the bullying or drama.

I have never seen a bully that was genuinely happy or had good self-confidence. He or she has always picked on others to boost their own self-worth which is usually temporary often resulting in a life-time pattern of unhappiness and abuse on others. If this identifies you, then I encourage you to find a more positive way to feel better about yourself. Change how you see yourself and don't hurt others in the process.

The mental and emotional scars resulting from bullying, if severe enough, can affect a person throughout their lifetime. Do not be that person responsible for inflicting life-long pain on someone else.

If your friends become too stressful to be around, you need to make better choices and find other friends or groups that can have a more positive impact in your life. It is ok to be supportive to your friends without becoming part of the problem; do not let it dominate your own life.

Remember, your friend's dramas are not necessarily your drama; if the drama negatively affects you and you are not directly involved, you need to stay out of it. If you are involved in the bullying of someone- you need to stop it now!

High school goes by very fast and you do not want to spend the majority of this exciting experience dealing with drama- there is too much fun to be had in high school than to waste your time on issues that do not directly involve you or that are really unimportant in the bigger picture.

Beware of friendships or relationships that:
- require total devotion and/or isolation.
- thrive on drama and gossip.
- discourage any friendships outside your established social group.
- monopolize your time away from your academics, other commitments, or your family.
- are more focused on using drugs and alcohol (partying) rather than on academic success and extracurricular activities.
- are disrespectful to you and/or your family. encourage you to give up things that you enjoy doing: sports, skateboarding, music, drama, gaming...
- encourage you to give up certain friends.

These types of friendships are toxic and are not examples of positive relationships. True friends should try to: make each other better persons, support each other's goals, enjoy being around each other, make each other laugh, and be low maintenance. (not too needy)

Straight from the Horse's Mouth

"Don't worry if some of your friends from middle school/high school change overtime and become people they weren't before. Focus on yourself and who you want to be around."

"If I could pass on something, I would say to always be aware of the effect they have on people, even with actions that were not intentional; be aware of the other's around you, notice how they are doing. It does not take much to ruin someone's day and it does not take much to make someone's day. A simple rude remark tends to be more memorable than a compliment, so try to make it easier with someone and fill them with all the kindness and compassion you can."

"Making new friends is never really hard, especially if you know yourself and know who you are; also, if you know the type of people you want to be surrounded by.

Getting involved is a great way to make new friends, being kind to everyone around you is also a great way. Like I said, it is not a challenge, but more so about letting the good ones come your way."

"To not worry about silly drama and focus on your school career. The most important thing about high school is getting your diploma, as well as staying satisfied while you are doing it. If you are more worried about the drama between friends while you are in class, why are you even in class?"

"I would change the people I started off with as my friends. This was a bad choice because they did not meet my standards. The people I hang out with now are not much into drama. If they are, I separate myself from that situation they put themselves in."

"My peers and I had pretty much the same vibe. We were simply stressed out, but very hopeful and determined to get the heck out of high school. I used to surround myself with bad influences, it caused me nothing but trouble, but making a change in friendships has honestly benefited me throughout the last year of high school. When the people around me are positive, I tend to be more positive."

Care enough about yourself to:

- **respect yourself first**, and be comfortable with who you are. Carry yourself with confidence, and try to make good choices.

- **create your own happiness.** Do not expect your boyfriends, girlfriends, family members or any others to create it for you. You are old enough to start relying on yourself.

- **surround yourself with positive, uplifting, fun and caring people.** Every day is an amazing opportunity for growth, both personally and educationally.

Start today by making each of your days better than the one before!

Chapter 12
Risky Behavior- Making Good Choices!

Making choices that are risky to your own health or the health of others is careless behavior. I have always told my students that in your decision-making process (should there be one), to weigh all of your options and possible outcomes, *before* you decide to act. If you determine that there is any possibility that even one of those outcomes could create potential harm to you or any other individual, don't do it!

What is a do-over?

I term a do-over as: the ability or chance of doing something over again with little or no permanent harm to oneself or to others. In other words: If there is even a slight chance that you or someone else may be harmed, altered in any way, then stop and move on!

I realize that many students do not think before they act in regards to careless behavior and the thought of permanent harm is too far reaching for many to consider. But, you are not invincible even at your age and unfortunately, the statistics prove it.

No "do-overs" cause life-changing events:
1) drinking to excess (alcohol poisoning) resulting in coma or death
2) very risky physical activity resulting in permanent injury or death
3) taking drugs- all levels and categories risking overdose, addiction or adverse reactions
4) having casual sex and contracting an STD such as herpes or becoming pregnant

Maybe you will get lucky the first, second, or even the third time you try something ... maybe not...

In regards to drugs, how often have you heard "the drugs of today are not like those of years ago?" If you doubt this statement, google the current drug-related death statistics and compare them to 10-20 years ago.

Who are these drug dealers? Drug dealers come in many shapes and sizes; they can be fellow students, strangers, neighbors, friends or even relatives. They are master manipulators, hustlers, and entrepreneurs. What they all have in common though is the sole purpose of "making money". They do not care who they sell to, what effects the drugs have on you or the outcome of your drug use. Drug dealers are unethical and illegal to the core.

Some drugs, like cocaine, are often <u>cut</u> (substances added to create more product that are similar in appearance) so that drug dealers can add weight or change the effects of the drug. The more weight, the more drugs to sell, the higher the profit. These substances used to cut cocaine often contain impurities which can be lethal to you, the end user. Substances added to cocaine range from using other drugs such as marijuana, LSD, PCP, to sugar, boric acid, and local anesthetics. This process of cutting is also done with many types of drugs so that you are not safe, regardless of your drug of choice.

Drug dealers do not care what happens to you! Who do you think drug dealers target? **You!** Why do you think they target the youth? You are young, naive and keep them in business longer! Who do drug dealers care about? **Themselves!**

An excellent YouTube video depicting real-life students who got caught up in the drug epidemic during high school is called "Overtaken". The follow-up documentary is called "Overtaken II." These documentaries were created and supported by the parents of these drug addicted students. Located in an upper middle class suburb in Southern California, some of these students were high academic achievers, some were athletes and some just got caught up in the drug scene. Each student was affected differently, but all paid a price that affected their future. I highly recommend that each and every incoming freshman and their parent(s) view these two videos. (see page 109)

In Health class, I have had numerous class discussions regarding drugs, alcohol and STD's. Many students were very forthcoming and wanted to discuss their personal habits and experiences, others chose to talk confidentially. The discussions during class were very enlightening to some students, uncomfortable for others. One student had experienced drug toxicity (lack of tolerance for the drug) which caused him to miss the following three months of school, another overdosed and was rushed to the hospital, and others say they had experienced no problems- **this time**.

*The drug epidemic is not a low class or poverty problem, it is **everyone's problem** happening in all economic levels of our high schools and filtering down into a growing number of middle schools across the United States.*

Brain chemical incompatibility, where the brain rejects a substance(s) inhaled, ingested or injected, is not uncommon and can result from just a one-time use. It can also happen on the 2nd, 3rd or 4th time using the same drug or in combination with other drugs. Who knows what the effect will be at that moment? Are you willing to risk it? Do you have a crystal ball? How happy will you be if your parent(s) have to take care of you the rest of your life because you tried some drug out of curiosity, or because your friends did it, or you gave-in to peer pressure? If your friends survived intact, why shouldn't you, right?

Although marijuana is legal in many states over the age of 21, it does not mean that it is not harmful particularly to an undeveloped brain (such as the high school age student or younger). Research has shown that a brain matures by around the age of 25 which means that high school and particularly middle school is way too early to be experimenting and changing your brain chemistry.

When it comes to drugs and alcohol, do not be a follower, do not bend to peer pressure or take your friend's word for it. You need to take responsibility for yourself! Practice being a critical thinker and educate yourself by doing your own research on the effects of drugs and alcohol on young brains. You may surprise yourself and find the results of your research life- altering in a positive direction. If you do not want to research, then look around you at the students at your school that may be using drugs, <u>you know who they are</u>.

Ask yourself: Do they have an apathetic attitude toward school or life in general? Do they excel academically? (some high achieving drug and alcohol users actually function fine "for a while") Were they good athletes, but now have little interest? Did they have big dreams and now are apathetic (do not care)? Do they seem happy? Are they content? Are they moody since they began using? Do they seem unusually depressed? Are they always tired? Have they gained or lost a large amount of weight?

The stories are endless, the risks are real. Do not waste your life by being a statistic, life is too precious! Please don't take chances that may permanently alter your brain chemistry and risk your future.

MAKE GOOD CHOICES AND SAFE DECISIONS!

It is human nature to want to hang around others that "do what you like to do"- good or bad.

Sometimes people hang out with friends that make poor decisions because it validates the poor decisions that they themselves make.

Sometimes we just make poor choices and get "stuck" in an environment that we need to remove ourselves from – that may require you to change some of your friends or groups.

Sometimes we may just get mixed up with the wrong crowd and struggle to get out- no friend or group is worth jeopardizing your own future!

Friends have limits and friendships can be temporary.

Straight from the Horse's Mouth

"Drugs have huge, tremendous mental and social impact on the kids in high school. Witnessing how my friends have changed due to the use of drugs has been absolutely horrifying to see. I had a friend who was the happiest, brightest, just all around greatest person I knew, and the moment she began to experiment with drugs, her life changed. She became depressed, her grades suffered, she gained a tremendous amount of weight, she withdrew from her friends, me included, she was a different person. And I see this all the time. Had I not changed, this would have been me. Had I not made a decision to do and be better, I would have been a different person than I am today. I look at it from many perspectives, and still, overall, I come to the same conclusion. It is so sad. I blame society and I blame the media."

"I think drugs have such a negative impact on campus. The freshmen are the ones that seem to be extremely affected by it, as I see more and more kids thinking they are 'all that because they do drugs. It is not cool."

"Drugs on high school campuses have become an epidemic. Each year seems to prove how widespread and normalized many drugs have become. Many kids try to boast and brag about their substance abuse. Where is zero tolerance? Fighting back this disease is a full-time job for any administration."

"If kids spent as much time on class assignments, studying on tests, researching future careers and even interning in interested areas rather than relying on social media and doing drugs for entertainment, then they could definitely be better prepared for a career, adulthood and ultimately supporting themselves."

"I find drugs mess kids up and prevents them from achieving their goals."

"I think vaping has become a real problem. I believe that this a problem worldwide. I have looked at articles of how there is more nicotine in these Juuls than there is in a pack of cigarette; using marijuana in these is another story. My friends go to it when they get stressed out. And I always think that is not the way to handle stress. You are not figuring out a healthy solution."

VIDEO RECOMMENDATIONS

There are an infinite number of videos on YouTube and Ted Talk that stand out regarding the issues affecting high schoolers and our young people today. It is impossible to list them all or to choose which videos are specific to your personal situation. Do your own research and preview the content to locate the best videos for your needs. I have listed below a few choice videos that I have shared with students that coincided to our lessons. Topics included: drug addiction, philosophy on a happy life, STD's and character, millennials in the workplace and a comedy on a millennnial interview. Feel free to share this information with others or additional videos that you have found during your own research.

- Ted Talk- My Philosophy for a Happy Life by Sam Burns (2013, 2018). An American teen who had a genetic disorder called progeria resulting in rapid premature aging (Benjamin Button disease). Sam's lecture is powerful and inspiring as he believes that no matter your obstacles, live a happy life.

- Overtaken Series: Documentary of real-life individual's stories regarding a California high school epidemic drug addiction and the price students paid due to their addiction. Overtaken Documentary (2012) [New]- about the ongoing prescription pill epidemic in Orange County, CA. • Overtaken 2- A follow-up of where are they now is the second documentary in the Overtaken series, dealing with the topics of addiction, sobriety, and hope in recovery.

• Pam Stenzel- A respected author, speaker and counselor regarding the price that is paid by young people that engage in risky behaviors and complications of contracting STD's. Character and Personality traits are discussed.
PAM STENZEL: "You Get What You Are"

• YouTube video by Simon Sinek, this is Why You Do Not Succeed, a motivational speech talking about Millennials in the workplace of today and our social media addiction dilemma. This 16' video is well worth your time to view for parents and students alike. Other videos by Simon Sinek: "Addiction to Technology is Ruining Lives – Simon Sinek on Inside... How to Make Your Life a Success... Simon Sinek on why you should put your phone away... How Do Cell Phones Impact Our ...".

• A Millennial Job Interview - YouTube:
(VID-20180123- WA0002.mp4) A millennial job interview comedy between a current employer and a millennial.

Chapter 13

Words of Wisdom
12 Key Thoughts to Remember Throughout Your High School Journey

1) Find your path and do not wait until it passes you by; explore different classes to see where your passion is strongest.

2) Whether you were a follower or leader in middle school, step up, maybe out of your comfort zone and try leadership roles in high school. This is an opportunity for you to explore and test your leadership skills, make new friends, and develop new passions.

3) No one is perfect; everyone makes mistakes. Do not blame someone else for your mistakes or what is your responsibility. Take responsibility, shoulder it, learn from it and move on. Develop and take pride in building a strong and honest character.

4) Don't sweat and stress over things you cannot control! It may be a waste of your time and energy that you could be placing in more positive areas.

5) Learn how to take tests, study ahead of time, not

only the night before. Reviewing class notes minimally 10-15 minutes each night (in addition to studying for tests) for each subject will help you with material retention and promote better test scores. Flash cards are a great tool for studying!

6) Do not procrastinate! It only encourages stress and lessens your work product.

7) Choose your friends carefully; not for popularity, but for how you can enrich each other's lives. Remember "character counts"!

8) Develop a strong support system of mentors and connect to others in your school and in your community.

9) Value yourself! Everyone matters and has their own gifts to share with others. Be kind to others and take time once a day to brighten someone else's life- the return is amazing!

10) Create a "healthy balance" in your life. Make time for academics, your physical, social and emotional health, and especially family time.

11) Remember that like most things in life, you get out of it what you put into it; your outcome can be dependent on the time and effort you are willing to dedicate to it.

12) Life is a constant learning curve- be flexible, be resilient and try not to be too hard on yourself! Life is too precious to waste and too fragile to leave behind.

Chapter 14

Straight from the Horse's Mouth
A Collection of Quotes and Reflections from Former High School Students

Straight from the Horse's Mouth is the title I have given to the series of quotes and reflections from former high school students. Their personal insights and lessons learned are listed by grade level, freshman through senior year, so that you can locate and read specific years or answers from those students at a specific grade level. The lessons learned at each grade level reflected their growing maturity, the numerous changes in their social circles, and the importance of school-focusing on their success after graduation. Pay attention to the senior quotes which are the most insightful and detailed as they have traveled the longest journey and have experienced the most growth and maturity through the previous four years.

The 5 questions asked and answered by high school students were:

1. The most valuable thing I learned this past year is-

2. As a _____ (your grade level), if I could change one thing or have a "do-over", what would it be?

3. Do you feel that it is easy to make new friends in high school?

4. What impact do you think phones are having in the classroom? Could you survive a day or two without your phone in class? Are phones interrupting your learning and ability to focus in class?

5. What effect do you think drugs have on your school campus and among your peers?

ADVICE FOR FRESHMEN

From Recent Freshmen

#1 The most valuable thing I learned this past year is-

"One lesson I learned and pass on to incoming freshman, is that high school will make you feel like it's every man for himself. You are going to lose a lot of friends, and people are busy with their own lives so you need to learn how to be your own support system, your own advocate, and be your own rock. Everyone's going to get into your business so you have to learn how to keep some things to yourself or else everyone will find out."

"To be responsible for myself. People won't try to keep me on task and help me, if I get a low grade, it is my job to work harder and do better."

"To stay out of people's business. What is NOT about me or even said to me is not meant for me to speak of. Teachers are not as soft as the ones in 8th grade; they don't care that you had practice or were sick the day before you have stuff to turn in or a test. Figure it out yourself!"

"I learned that it is hard to find a good group of friends and also not to allow things to bother me so much."

"Some lessons would be: cut out toxic friends, just do your work, don't procrastinate, and bring lunch every day."

"To speak up and not to be shy around teachers and friends. To raise your hand to answer questions and to do all of your homework so you don't get behind. Also, to study for tests and to read the book your supposed to read for English."

"I would not slack off so much and try harder with my grades than I already do."

"That high school isn't just about having fun and goofing off." I learned to always stay focused and to never slack because it is harder to get back up than it is to fall."

"Don't wait until the last minute; once you fall in a hole, the hole keeps getting deeper, so you better dig yourself out sooner than later."

"Make sure to start off your year with a small real circle of friends, friends that mean the most to you and have showed you that they have no wrong intentions.

Stay with the 4-5 friends that make you happy and have showed loyalty. Trust me, high school is full of drama and you have a choice to be in that or not."

"I had to take 7th period this semester to make up my class I failed first semester. I regretted not doing my work when it was due."

"I would have worked a little harder to get the A in every single class instead of settling for a B."

"Not to fail Math and to pay attention."

"We are in high school only for so long. Don't care about what other people think of you and have fun while you are still a teenager. No one's going to remember you in 10 years except a few good friends."

"High school may make you feel like it's every man for himself. You're going to lose a lot of friends, and people are busy with their own lives, so you need to learn how to be your own support system and be your own rock." Everyone's going to get into your business so you have to learn how to keep some things to yourself or else everyone will find out."

"Make sure to pick your own classes and do your community service hours."

"Choose your friends wisely; the people you hang around with are the people you become because this affects your education and how you learn."

"Some advice I could offer to some incoming freshmen is to begin focusing on yourself. Stop caring about being the most "popular" in school. It won't benefit you in life. Hang around the people who are better than you. The people around you will begin to influence you and your future. Also, stop complaining about your shortcomings in life."

"To always focus and work hard on your school work and quality over quantity. Education should be your top priority, I also learned that a few close friends is better than a lot of friends/acquaintances."

"Hang around people that have the same interests as you."

"Pay attention in class and not to mess around because it did not help me all throughout first semester."

"Never stop trying. Have a good attitude and be optimistic. If you push through with the bare minimum, it won't get you very far; but if you give it your all, you are guaranteed to do good."

"Not to waste time and to pay attention in class. I learned these two lessons in Math class. I had not paid attention to the lesson and I wasted time afterwards trying to figure out how to do the math. After that, I pay attention to all of my lessons and complete any work I get right away."

"To surround yourself with people who you know you can trust and do all of your work ASAP and turn it in as soon as you are done, that way you are able to do extra-curricular activities whenever you want, don't ask."

"You should never take for granted your grades. Because, near the end of the year, a lot of homework was given out and if you slack off, your grade could drop even at the final."

"Yes, I have learned that I can influence the younger kids. If they see me doing something good or bad, it could influence a younger kid to do the same."

"No matter what happens, you should always keep trying no matter what the situations is."

"I learned two lessons: First that you should work hard on your grades because the transition from middle to high school is very hard and slacking off can lead to you not doing other activities. Second, is learn to be more independent and stop depending on people to do things for me."

"One of the most valuable lessons I learned was to not give up, because better things are around the corner. And not to stress so much because everyone's going through something- you are not the only one."

"That even when things get difficult, you can't give up."

"The people you walk in with are probably not the people you will walk out with and you don't need to stress out about that. They should know that people change once they get into high school because there are a lot of new people and people try new things. You will lose friends, but you will gain friends as well. Another lesson is, everything is going to be okay; things happens, friendships end, relationships end, and you will be thrown through a lot of hoops, but it's all worth it in the long run."

"To focus on yourself and your responsibilities as well as learn to be more independent. As a young person, people tend to rely on others to do everything for them and guide them all the way until they succeed, but high school gives you a new perspective which allows you to see what it will be like in the future. I need to put myself first, but this is no way means I've stopped caring for anyone in my life, it just means I need to take care of myself above all else."

"The biggest mistake that freshmen make is constantly on a daily basis is that they believe that senior year is far away from today but the issue is that they do not realize the fact that a year feels like a month and a month feels like a week. Time is flying out of our grasp and they have no come to realize that this is reality and we are becoming adults."

"Don't hold yourself back from doing things. I feel like we get so caught up in our school work, that we allow it to take away from our time we have as kids. Our time in high school is very limited due to college. So, try not to let yourself or others hold you back. Enjoy the time you have with your friends, and don't stress about the little things in life."

"The most important thing that I have learned this year is that I see school differently than I used to. I used to think of school as a horrible, mandatory thing that everyone needed to do. I didn't used to like having to go to school, but now I see school as a fun place where I can learn information, make friends, and exercise. I no longer enjoy having to go home. I played football in my first semester, ran track and field for my second semester and now I am training for cross country next year. I joined these sports not only to have fun and exercise, but to spend less time at home and more time at school."

#2 As a Freshman, if I could change one thing or have a do-over, what would it be?

"It would be how much effort I put into my school work. I wish I could undo how unproductive I was and how much I would procrastinate."

"I would begin to study more and try harder to pay attention in class and focus on my personal life less."

"I would have changed the people that I hung around with."

"For me to focus more first semester. I should have paid more attention in class and do my work. My grades were better second semester because I paid attention and did my work."

"It would definitely be my work habits and how I handled school work throughout football season."

"I would be more involved with the high school activities that go on and have gone to more events."

"The most valuable lesson I learned this year was that grades really matter and to give it your all with them and try your hardest. It will benefit you down the road and make you a better student and person. I would also say that friends come and go and find the ones who really stick with you and go out of their way for you. Last, I would say to not get into the bad things, you will get caught and have bad outcomes."

"If I got to change one thing about this year, I would try to prepare myself even better for exams and finals that are coming up and balance my life more thoroughly between school and sports."

"My do over this year would be to take my math class more seriously and get way more help than I did."

"Do all my work in class and ask more question than I originally did. I did not meet my own expectations nor my parents."

"I would try to enjoy school activities more such as: dances, football games and participate in Spirit Days."

"I would change how my grades were first semester; I would change some of the things I have done this year because I have done a lot of things I am not proud of…"

"I was absent quite a bit and so in return, I had some missing assignments. I needed to take care of my business."

"If I had to change one thing about this year would probably be my friend group. Over this past year, I have been through a lot, but it has also taught me a lot. I went through a devastating heartbreak, with not only my ex-boyfriend, but also my best friend. I made new friends and I can honestly say I have never been happier. They have taught me what friendship really is and I am so beyond thankful for my new friends."

"I wouldn't change anything about this school year because I have the friends I wanted, I keep a somewhat small circle but full of meaningful friends that have stuck around with me for a long time and showed the real type of friend they are."

"One thing I would do-over would be to have my attitude turned down a little but, turned in my homework as I have noticed how it has affected my grades and citizenship."

"I would have joined more clubs and joined a sports team. I did not think I had enough time, but I could have fit it in."

"I would change the people I started off with as my friends. This was a bad choice because they did not meet my standards. The people I hang out with now are not much into drama. If they are, I separate myself from that situation they put themselves in."

"I probably should have put in more effort. I didn't really show up for school very often and didn't try the best on my assignments when I knew I could do better. I slacked off in hopes of being able to switch schools but that just backfired."

"I would have stopped myself from talking with fake and toxic people."

"I would try to break out of my shell faster and talk to more people."

#3 Do you feel that it is easy to make new friends in high school?

"Yes, there are people at schools for everyone. There are so many people with different personalities, character, interests and hobbies, sports, academics…that you bond to kind people just like you."

"The fact that high school has many different age groups has really made it easier to make friends with not only freshmen, but with upperclassmen as well. I really feel as though having some friends who are older than you can be quite beneficial, allowing you to find the right maturity group and preparing yourself for years to come."

"It has never been easy making friends in middle or elementary school. I had friends, but they were always mean to me by bullying me, making fun of me and pretending to be my friend; but, when I got to high school, I made great friends who are nice to me and make me laugh and smile instead of making me cry which is good. I love the friends I have now."

"My group has a lot of fun together; we are always focused on our work and strive for what we want to be or what we're going to do in the future. We are not competitive with one another, but support everyone's goals. If you ever see my group, you will always see us smiling or laughing because they are just good people to be around."

"You can always switch groups or have multiple friends from many groups."

"It really depends on what kind of person you are. If you are funny and happy, you can make a lot of your fellow classmates your friends."

"It is much easier in high school because there are more students. Some may be perfect to be your friend and you may meet others that are maybe better off as acquaintances."

"There are a lot of groups in high school that are separated and standoffish toward one another. If more groups joined together than people would have more friends and more people to talk to all the time."

"I think it is easy if you are kind and open minded. There are many clubs that you can join according to your interests and that can be your ticket to earn friends who like the same things you do."

"I found that new friends also introduce you to new people too."

"Yes, I just make sure to make the right friends and talk to the right people in high school about the right things."

#4 What impact do you think phones are having in the classroom? Could you survive a day or two without your phone in class? Are phones interrupting your learning and ability to focus in class?

"Kids not having phones in the classroom is better because then kids have to interact with one another and that will help you make new friends. I can survive as long as I want without my phone in class. When I listen to my phone, it helps me to relax and really think about what I am doing in class."

"Now that phones are allowed on campus, I feel that they have made a big impact. People are now so distracted and seem to believe that it is ok to use their phones whilst the teacher is trying to teach. I do not personally feel that it has personally affected my learning and ability to focus because I try not to abuse the privilege."

"I think phones can impact negatively and positively. Phones can be used to distract students from work because of their social networks. They can also be used educationally."

"The impact of having phones in the classroom either disrupts or continues the ability of people to work; some students will not put their phones away regardless."

"Phones are crazy... in class I hardly survive without my phone. I do not care as much about text, but music helps me concentrate and get through the day."

"Phones are a good think to have in the classroom because students can look up information right away and have access to things like a calculator and a dictionary. Occasionally phones can be distracting in classrooms if the ringer is on or if someone constantly checked their phone."

#5 What effect do you think drugs have on your school campus and among your peers?

"Drugs are not having a good effect on my peers. I feel that they stop caring about everything but when they are going to get high again."

"I think drugs are having a negative impact on students because they are getting in more trouble and also they are convincing other kids to do drugs."

"Drugs are affecting not only attendance of students at school, but also their work habits and how they treat their fellow peers and their teachers."

"I think that some students think it's a way to get out of their depression and it's sad that they rely on that for happiness. Doing drugs is just going to make things worse in the long run. They can be depressed again when one thing they once relied on to be happy is gone. They have to develop healthy coping mechanisms to deal rather than to do drugs."

"Drugs are always bad and is definitely a no go." (Recreational drugs, that is)

"Drugs are affecting our campus because students don't care and think that they are cool; but when it comes to them getting caught, they get mad saying that it is not their fault when they personally brought them to school."

"I think drugs has had a big impact on our campus. I know for a fact that many students are using drugs to escape their worries. I really don't know how to support these students or encourage better behavior because it seems as though we have done everything we can; it is up to them whether or not they want to stop."

"Drugs are everywhere. Not hard to get but difficult to afford on a regular basis. Waste of money."

ADVICE FOR SOPHOMORES

From Recent Sophomores

#1 The most valuable thing I learned this past year is-

"Never stop trying. Have a good attitude and be optimistic. If you push through with the bare minimum, it won't get you very far; but if you give it your all, you are guaranteed to do good."

"I learned that you cannot let your comrades interfere with your work habits and persistence throughout the year. It is good to have friends, but not those who are distracting and prevent you from performing at your highest potential. If I had to pass on one thing to incoming sophomores, it is to know who your good friends are who will not only accompany you, but motivate you to be the best version of yourself."

"This year of high school was a lot more than I expected. I thought sophomore year was going to be as easy as freshman year, but it was harder and I got caught slipping."

"To work hard on every assignment and just do your work. Be nice to everyone you meet even if you do not like them because one day you might need them."

"Think carefully about your course selection, your friends may be taking it, but it may not be the right fit for you."

#2 As a sophomore, if I could change one thing or have a do-over, what would it be?

"During my two years of high school, the one thing I would change is realizing things sooner. I learned and realized things about myself in which I am a very different person compared to the person I started off the school year."

"To do better in Biology and Geometry because I worked very hard first semester and played sports. Then second semester came and I kind of stopped working hard and did not really want to work anymore."

"My work ethics. I had an awful work ethic going into this year, but improved it as I went out. My bad work ethic caused me to fall behind in some classes and fail more than I'd like."

"This year was a lot harder than freshman year. I wish that I had been more serious about my grades last year as I had a lot to catch up on, especially in math and English."

"I wish that I spent more time on school than with my friends. They did not care as much as I did."

#3 Do you feel that it is easy to make new friends in high school?

"I think that it is pretty easy to make friends if you just be yourself."

"It's easy to make friends because if you have the same class, if we both need help, a friend relationship could happen in a matter of seconds and then you have something in common to start off with."

"You need to be open-minded when meeting new people."

"I am more confident this year than freshman year. I am ready to join some clubs which will help me to make more friends."

"I am new to this school from out of state. When I joined a sports team it gave me a set of friends."

#4 What effect do you think drugs have on your school campus and among your peers?

"Drugs affect campuses by reducing the ability for us to think properly."

"Drugs can either confuse or lead to memory loss and these people will have problems when they are older."

"They may or may not be able to focus during class, it has a different effect on everybody."

"With drugs at our school, I cannot say much because I do not associate with people of that kind. I really am on a path that only I will understand and my goal is to succeed for myself and god. Therefore, I stay away from people that associate with drugs because we obviously do not have the same mind set and future goals."

"I think that drugs on our campus is a danger to learning because kids who are addicted to it could be unfocused on what they are doing because they are high or need to get high."

"Most of my peers advanced and tightened themselves up compared to last year. They seem more focused. Some people I didn't really know well became more into the wrong things like drugs and alcohol. They can care less about life or education."

ADVICE FOR JUNIORS

From Recent Juniors

#1 The most valuable thing I learned this past year is-

"Don't procrastinate!"

"I would probably tell younger students to always study and complete work so it doesn't end up hurting them later on in the semester."

"Make your life fun by being involved in sports, school activities and friends."

"Through the years, I have learned many valuable life lessons. I've learned to stay organized, not to procrastinate and also to keep on top of all my work because college you do not get to turn in work late and they are way stricter so high school has definitely helped me prepare."

"The vibes I got this year is very focused. As juniors, it has been very important for us to get our stuff together because we will soon be applying to college. This is the year to be focused."

"Make friends in your classes as everyone helps each other."

"To never miss much school and to never slack off because you will be ending up getting a bad grade for the class."

"Do your work, it really helps, even if it is just a meaningless worksheet, just get it done. Focus is important."

"It feels like there is more drama nowadays involving the use of technology which negatively affects people's relationships whether it be friends or a significant other."

"I have learned that people should really enjoy as much as they can when in high school because even though many people say this, high school goes by really fast whether you are having a great time or not. Another thing I would like to share is "not to do stupid things with friends"; you can be better than that. Even though you might be tempted to try something, don't do it as it could really have life-long effects. Your future is at jeopardy especially if the results do not offer a "do- over."

"Always aim for high grades and always do the work."

"Take school very seriously if you are an athlete because you will have a better chance of playing college sports as scholarships are very competitive."

"My junior year has been very challenging in many different ways. This year, I have overcome several obstacles I did not realize I would have to overcome. Some of these obstacles would include: difficult tests, registration for these tests, as well as the workload that was overwhelming."

"The most valuable lesson I learned this year was to always believe in yourself, trust yourself, take care of yourself, and most importantly, love yourself. I would tell other younger students that because if we continue to put ourselves down and never believe we can achieve a certain goal, we will never survive what the future brings."

#2 As a Junior, if I could change one thing or have a do-over, what would it be?

"If I could change one thing this year, or could have a do-over, it would probably be focus more on my grades. I spent a lot of time not worrying about the outcome of my grades but I know now I really should have."

"I would have taken this year a lot more seriously. I did not push myself enough."

"I wished that I could prevent myself from procrastinating on all of my work, if I did the, the efficiency of the finished work would improve dramatically grade-wise."

"I might have tried to meet more people and make more friends."

"I would change the amount of time I spent doing homework because I didn't do any of my homework."

"I would tell them to do all of your work and study hard because you will have a lot of work junior year."

"If I could change one thing this year is to not date or have relationships because it became very labor-intensive, emotionally draining which took away and distracted me from my school work. Having lots of "friends" was a better way to go."

"To not worry about silly drama and focus on your school career. The most important thing about high school is getting your diploma, as well as staying satisfied while you are doing it. If you are more worried about the drama between friends while you are in class, why are you even in class?"

"If I had to change one thing about this year, I would change that time where I met the most toxic people who broke me and put me to the edge. I wish I knew better than sticking up for them when all they did was make me feel insecure and made me feel bad about myself. I wish I cut them off sooner because they were not very positive. Making new positive friends make the difference. Start by being kinds and find people who seem very open and very friendly."

#3 Do you feel that it is easy to make new friends in high school?

"I believe it isn't too hard to make new friends in high school. I feel like you just can't be too shy. You have to make yourself more outgoing so people aren't naturally turned away from you."

"Just be yourself is the best way to find true friends."

"Yes, personally I felt it was easy to make friends because I went up to so many people and introduced myself and a lot of people respected me for that."

"I feel it's easier at the beginning of the year to make friends as it goes on, people become set in their groups."

"Just a 'hello' can lead to a million positive things."

#4 What impact do you think phones are having in the classroom? Could you survive a day or two without your phone in class? Are phones interrupting your learning and ability to focus in class?

"Phones can have a positive influence and a negative influence in the classroom. Good for looking up information, but negative in the classroom as they take away learning from the students as it takes away from learning and they fall behind on their studies."

"The impact phones are having in the classroom is high. You never not see kids without a phone which makes it not only difficult for the student to focus and learn, but also for the teacher to teach a group of kids who are not paying attention."

"Phones can be a positive or negative. I know many students who have used social media to hurt someone they are jealous of. Your school can track the source and then you get into a lot of trouble. My freshman year was worse on social media, but it got better when kids were getting caught. Don't be hurtful!"

"I think phones are having a good impact on the student in the classroom. Students listen to their music to stay on task and not distract each other."

"I think phones are a great tool to be used to either research or do a quick calculation."

"Phones in general can be a very big distraction as it pushes me back from doing my work and then I do everything last minute."

"I feel like phones make us not socialize with the people in our classrooms because we are so focused on our screen instead of our surroundings. Personally, I do not think I could survive a day without my phone due to the many friendships I have with people online, as silly as it sounds, unless I could meet them in person, then yes. I do feel like phones interrupt over 50% of people's learning and ability to focus in class because it realistically makes us absorbed on the internet or on a text message we should really be focusing in class."

"I could do without my phone, just not without my music."

#5 What effect do you think drugs have on your school campus and among your peers?

"Drugs on campus don't affect anyone but the drug user, so it does not affect me or my classmates. All you can do is ask them to stop, but they do not care what you say."

"The effects I see with drugs is they are getting bigger."

"Drugs change people; people I grew up with are not the same people as they were after having taken drugs."

"I feel just like phones, drugs can become very addictive once you get a taste for it. Many students have bad addictions due to major influences in their life including family, friends, money and school."

"I had to change friend groups because I was starting to fail my classes; that's not me."

"It was fun for a while, but I couldn't keep up with anything."

"I had fun for a while, but then lost track of who I was. It was a hard lesson, but now I'm good."

ADVICE FOR SENIORS
From Recent Seniors

These lessons learned are very insightful and heartfelt as these students traveled through and completed their very own 4-Year Journey.

#1 The most valuable lesson I learned this past year is –

"I have learned how important it is to have a support system. Make connections with your most personable teachers. Make friends in all of your classes. Be nice to everyone and anyone you come across, because kindness matters."

"Being a senior I have learned a lot about friends and school. I am not the best to consult but it's some advice: I would just say to really get those A's in your early years because it'll get you some places and awards. Connect with the community as well and become well-rounded. But remember, the school is making you 'so-well rounded' that no one truly knows what they are passionate for. So, find one thing you'll like and truly love to doing and stick to it... As for friends, they'll come and go…it's up to your own morals on how to decide on whether you want to be around them… also to hang out with them as much as possible... Take your chances, believe me. It'll be worth it."

"As a senior this year, I would like to pass on an important message to my younger peers, or to anyone who is starting out in high school. My message is this: Take high school and make it the best experience that you possible can. Focus on your schoolwork and studies, yes, but never forget to enjoy life and enjoy yourselves. That was my biggest mistake...getting too caught up in schoolwork, stressing myself out, that I did not get to enjoy the years or myself."

"I would like to see more passion and determination. Our generation lacks passion. It is so hard to find students who can genuinely say that they love something enough to the point that they would fight for it, fight against what others say, and fight for it with integrity. Our generation needs to be stronger mentally; we are very weak. As it is seen multiple times, whenever we do not get what we want, we throw a fit, we lash out and we feel entitled. That needs to change. We need to understand the harsh reality of life. That in after high school, things do not always go our way; things are not handed to us. The more we are enabled, the less likely we will be able to succeed on our own. That need to change."

"The most valuable lesson I could give out to others as I graduate is the fact that being social will get you long ways. Reason being is because coming from my experience, I became more social and more interactive and wanting to meet new people. Those new people I have met changed my life definitely with who I have become as a person and what I strive to do in the future. (EMT)"

"Each year in high school I had faced different vibes and experiences because there was a lot going on in each of those years. For example; freshman year I was very nervous on fitting in and finding new styles of clothing and such but also very determined in working out as well as I had finally signed up for a gym membership that year. Sophomore year I had found my first love and I felt like nothing else mattered, I was so happy and adored in my girlfriend. Junior year came along and with the reality where choices in finding a job and balancing the gym and hanging out with my friends and girlfriend became difficult. Senior year came and I lost my love as she wanted someone new but I was positive and felt free and I was happy again, striving for new goals and new desires of who I actually am as a person to set all these goals for my career in the medical field."

"I have a lot of little brothers and my number one line of advice is not to count yourself out. I missed out on a lot of things that could have helped me make connections just because I wanted to "look cool" but looking back I missed a lot of great opportunities."

"High School flies by so fast so don't let anything or anyone get to you. Stay positive and work your hardest. Things pass by and so do people so while in the present, you feel like you won't make it, you will! This is just a minor bump in your future. Don't dwell on anything too much; you are too good for that! The only thing you will regret is not trying your hardest now."

"The most valuable lesson that I have learned in my four years it to always try. No matter how hard the class material is, or no matter how hard the teacher grades, you CANNOT get frustrated and pull away from the material and give up on the class. Make the deadlines. Do the homework. Pay attention. Just try. School is not hard unless you make it that way for yourself."

"As a senior, I have learned that it is important to communicate to those around you. And communication is not only talking, but also listening. Younger students should understand that their counselors have helped many students with various problems, their teachers are well-educated and versed in their subjects, and many of their peers are always willing to help one another out. With this being said, younger students should not be afraid to ask questions or for help and should always be willing to listen."

"Research career options so that I could select courses more focused on my choice(s). Course exposure in those fields could help me in college courses."

"Don't hold yourself back from doing things. I feel like we get caught up in our school work, that we allow it to take away from our time we have as kids. Enjoy the time you have with your friends, and don't stress about the little things in life."

"I feel that vibes change as each student goes through the four years of high school. Freshman year they start off nervous, drama obsessed, and uptight. Sophomore year they slowly start to break out of their comfort shell, and by Junior year, they become more focused on getting good grades because they have to start thinking about the colleges they want to get into. Lastly, by senior year I feel like we become more relaxed, and stress less."

"The most important thing I learned over the year is that procrastination is always joked about but it truly will kill your grades, sleep and stress levels. If you have work that is due in a week, do it the day you get it so you have the rest of the week to relax instead of the day before. Early done work is good and you can make sure to go back and make it perfect. Rushed work is not great work."

"Senior year is a little of everything; excited to graduate, nervous to be an adult, senioritis, scared and maybe depressed."

"Stay on task. Try to balance things out between having fun and getting your education. If you work hard now, you will be thanking yourself in the long run."

"Some valuable things that I have learned throughout my four years of high school that I would like to pass on is that you are going to miss all of the shots you do not take. Personally, there is so much that I should have done or experienced throughout high school that I chose not to and I honestly regret it. Whether it was taking a harder class to push myself or just something as simple as going to a football game with my friends, those are things that I am not going to get to do in high school anymore because those are the shots I never took."

"Valuable things that I have learned is that excellence has to be a habit if I expect to get anywhere in life. I also learned that hard work sucks but has its rewards. Finally, I learned a few small things about life through growing up and maturing."

"If I could pass on something, I would say to always be aware of the effect they have on people, even with actions that were not intentional; be aware of the other's around you, notice how they are doing. It does not take much to ruin someone's day and it does not take much to make someone's day. A simple rude remark tends to be more memorable than a compliment, so try to make it easier with someone and fill them with all the kindness and compassion you can."

"The most valuable lesson I have seriously learned is to just keep on persevering, no matter what."

"Don't be fake. Playing football or being attractive has nothing to do with being cool. Being yourself and proud will be cooler than anyone that has to fake themselves to the top. It's not about having a lot of friends, but how deep a connection with another person is better than a bunch of people. And start focusing on career choices. Then afterwards, look at majors that will build your career."

"Throughout my senior year, I have experienced and seen many forms of expressions. Stress, excitement, focus, and sadness were the primary things I have felt. Stress for those who don't know what they want to do after high school or they are afraid they won't graduate. Excitement to leave high school and enter the real world. Focus to make sure they pass and get ready for college, and sadness for those who know they will never experience this event again in their lives."

#2 As a Senior, if I could change one thing or had a 'do- over' what would it be?

"My peers and I had pretty much the same vibe. We were simply stressed out, but very hopeful and determined to get the heck out of high school. I used to surround myself with bad influences, it caused me nothing but trouble, but making a change in friendships has honestly benefited me throughout the last year of high school. When the people around me are positive, I tend to be more positive."

"I wish I took school more seriously in the beginning. Because I knew I hated school, it took a toll on my grades so I limited myself and projected an image that made me look a lot less intelligent than I really am."

"Don't let 'senioritis' destroy all the good grades you worked hard on for the past four years."

"I gave up second semester and I am deeply disappointed in myself. My GPA has hit the lowest it's ever been. I can't take it back, but I can continue to do my work."

"If I could change one thing it would be to participate in more school events. I would try to go to the little things I thought weren't going to be fun or I thought that no one would go with me and I missed so much."

"I would change the fact that I piled too many things (classes and activities) on my schedule that I ended up struggling a lot more than I needed to."

"If I had to change one thing throughout my senior year, it would be to not let anyone hold you back. I feel as though I have held myself back from doing things inside and outside of school, such as going to more football games, participating in school events, and going out with my friends more."

"If I could do this year over, I would have started out with a better attitude and with more confidence in myself. I cared so much what people thought of me and now that the year in coming to an end, I can see now how little the opinions of others about me matter. I wish I had just been myself and been able to surround myself with better people."

"I wish that I would have started off with the attitude that I ended with. I made many mistakes this year that made my year a lot harder. I lost friends and gained many. The friends I lost were toxic and I didn't realize it until 2nd semester. However, the ones I gained are those that will carry me to the end."

"I would change nothing in particular for this year honestly. There were good times and bad, but whatever has happened, it is all part of life and it has definitely contributed to who I am today in some sort of shape or form, regardless of the events of my life that have taken place this year."

"If I could change one thing about this year it would be to take away any drama that I was involved with and to stay out of it, even if it included me. If I did this, I would have been a lot less stressed and a lot happier. However, it happened and I learned from it, so I would not necessarily change it."

#3 Do you feel that it is easy to make new friends in high school?

"Making new friends is never really hard, especially if you know yourself and know who you are; also, if you know the type of people you want to be surrounded by. Getting involved is a great way to make new friends, being kind to everyone around you is also a great way. Like I said, it is not a challenge, but more so about letting the good ones come your way."

"Being around people who understand you and like you for you is what makes it easy to make friends."

"Don't worry if some of your friends from middle school/high school change overtime and become people they weren't before. Focus on yourself and who you want to be around."

"It is very easy to make 'friends' but it is very hard to make 'true' friends. You just have to go into the friendship guarding yourself and keeping your personal things to yourself, at least until you establish if they are 'true' friends."

"Acceptance and open mindedness will make making friends easier."

"Getting involved in clubs such as PEER leaders, ASB, SADD, HOSA, and any club that helps others often has many activities that help you to integrate and be more inclusive on campus."

"I have always had a harder time making friends (more me than anyone else) until my summer going into my junior year. I attended a leadership conference over the summer where it taught me to break out of my comfort shell and show off who I really am. To make it easier, I think you should try not to be afraid of what others think of you, if they don't like you, that is on them, not you."

"Senior year was actually a year of either reconnecting with old friends, making new friends, or doing both. For me it was both, and looking back on my years I wish I had done it earlier."

"It is not always easy to make friends. People can be rude and 'too cool' to welcome you into their friend group. People are way too quick to judge and spread rumors, and we are often all guilty of these things. Being nice is not any longer a cool thing. People who are constantly making fun of others and involved in drama and drugs are usually the most popular."

"It is easy to make new friends in high school as long as you come into it with a positive attitude. As long as you smile and be uplifting, then finding friends isn't too hard."

#4 What impact do you think phones are having in the classroom? Could you survive a day or two without your phone in class? Are phones interrupting your learning and ability to focus in class?

"Phones and technology impede learning in my opinion. Phones are a distraction to nearly everyone on campus, and nationwide. Society is becoming accustomed to new technology and all of the advances, that it seems to be a necessity. This needs to change."

"I believe there has to be a better balance in teaching and students using their phones."

"Phones are the reason why students are not being involved in the classroom. Social media is becoming more and more addicting and hard to get away from. People also worry too much about social media like how many followers they may have or how many likes they get on their posts."

"Teachers believe that phones are a distraction but, in reality, it's helping student more than they think. It is a great tool when chrome books are not available."

"Phones can get very distracting sadly. Honestly, I don't know if I could go without my phone in my classes I have just gotten accustomed to always having it and checking it every so often. Earphones personally help me focus but can also help me to block out lectures when I don't want to listen which is negative."

"Phones in the classroom has become a HUGE issue. Many kids are glued to it therefore not listening and unable to set it down. Distraction and frustration can affect teachers and students alike."

"I feel that phones become a big distraction inside and outside the classroom. I am guilty of it, I become distracted by music or what is going on social media and what not. However, I could definitely survive a day or two without my phone in class. In fact, I feel that it would be beneficial because I would become more focused."

"Phones are not the problem, it is the constant need for attention due to social media and messaging. People are too worried about what people think rather than focusing on the important thing... SCHOOL; Yes, phones are extremely distracting."

"I think phones are distracting to students but I also think that it can be a tool for learning or finding out new things. I think it would be hard to not have my phone for a day or two because it is a means of communication for me and my loved ones. I do think that phones are interrupting my ability to focus on school because anytime I hear my phone buzz, I want to look at who is on the notification."

"Technology is so convenient now. I have had to clean up my social media sites when I started to apply to colleges and hoped they did not see my previous posts. I wish I had thought or known about it freshman year."

#5 What effect do you think drugs have on a school campus and among your peers?

"Drugs have huge, tremendous mental and social impact on the kids in high school. Witnessing how my friends have changed due to the use of drugs has been absolutely horrifying to see. I had a friend who was the happiest, brightest, just all around greatest person I knew, and the moment she began to experiment with drugs, her life changed. She became depressed, her grades suffered, she gained a tremendous amount of weight, she withdrew from her friends, me included, she was a different person. And I see this all the time. Had I not changed, this would have been me. Had I not made a decision to do and be better, I would have been a different person than I am today. I look at it from many perspectives, and still, overall, I come to the same conclusion. It is so sad. I blame society and I blame the media."

"Drugs are what's wrong with students today. Students feel it is cool to do drugs if others are doing them too and they get to the point where drugs are an everyday thing. Students come to school high and have no idea what is going because they're in a different world."

"The drug problem is obnoxious in high school. Out of all the places, kids have to come to school with them; it's absurd and to change this behavior is a huge process and I believe it will take years and a lot of education to decrease this problem."

"Drugs on high school campuses have become an epidemic. Each year seems to prove how widespread and normalized many drugs have become. Many kids try to boast and brag about their substance abuse. Where is zero tolerance? Fighting back this disease is a full-time job for any administration."

"I think drugs have such a negative impact on campus. The freshmen are the ones that seem to be extremely affected by it, as I see more and more kids thinking they are 'all that' because they do drugs. It is not cool."

"If kids spent as much time on class assignments, studying on tests, researching future careers and even interning in interested areas rather than relying on social media and doing drugs for entertainment, then they could definitely be better prepared for a career, adulthood and ultimately supporting themselves."

"I find drugs mess kids up and prevents them from achieving their goals."

"I think vaping has become a real problem. I believe that this a problem worldwide. I have looked at articles of how there is more nicotine in these Juuls than there is in a pack of cigarettes; using marijuana in these is another story. My friends go to it when they get stressed out. And I always think that is not the way to handle stress. You are not figuring out a healthy solution."

CHAPTER 15
Conclusion

Your experience in high school is twofold. First and foremost, it is to gain an education that you can build on to create your own future. You will take away from it exactly the effort you put into it. Secondly, it is to mature and establish relationships with peers, teachers and within your community in preparation for the adult world. Challenge yourself to become involved in school clubs, sports, academic competitions or whatever stimulates your interests and contributes toward your goals. As you mature, you will gain in self-confidence.

Explore outside of your comfort zone from time to time and reach out to other positive peers that you may not normally introduce yourself to or associate with. You might be pleasantly surprised at what you have in common.

As a teacher, our role has expanded well beyond just teaching knowledge. We are also role models, mentors, listeners and cheerleaders for our students encouraging each and every one of you to become life-long learners, scholars, leaders, critical thinkers, and good citizens.

Final Words of Wisdom:
- Each one of you control your own path- the

more you engage in all aspects of high school, the more enriched your high school journey and life will become.

- Set your goals high. You might surprise yourself at what you have accomplished.

- Push yourself to be the best you can be!

- Find and identify your support system early on in high school so that you know who and where you can reach out to for help if necessary.

- Believe in yourself, trust your instincts and do not compromise your values and morals.

- Follow your passions, interests and goals and most importantly, be happy and enjoy your life.

- If you can dream it, believe you can achieve it.

- The world is yours for the taking and anything is possible with hard work, resilience and perseverance! Make your high school journey one of the most exciting chapters of your life.

NOW GO CREATE YOUR OWN

FOOTPRINT

AND DESIGN YOUR OWN MEMORABLE

SNAPSHOTS!

www.ingramcontent.com/pod-product-compliance
Lightning Source LLC
Chambersburg PA
CBHW071401290426
44108CB00014B/1635